LAKE SUPERIOR

Mississippi River

LAKE HURON

LAKE MICHIGAN

Wisconsin River

Des Moines River

Illinois River

Wabash River

LAKE ERIE

LAKE ONTARIO

Hudson River

CAPE COD

LONG ISLAND

ALLEGHENY MOUNTAINS

Delaware River

Potomac River

CHESAPEAKE BAY

Missouri River

Ohio River

OZARK PLATEAU

Mississippi River

APPALACHIAN MOUNTAINS

Savannah River

CAPE HATTERAS

Tennessee River

PIEDMONT PLATEAU

Chattahoochee River

ATLANTIC OCEAN

Mississippi River

GULF OF MEXICO

Lake Okeechobee

FLORIDA KEYS

917.3   Time-Life
Tim   Library of nations: United States.
Hughes   Time-Life Books, 1984.
c.4   160 p.   photos (pt. col.)
               Bibliography: p. 156-157.

           1. United States - Description and
           travel. I. Title.

50238249   86-1469/15.00/add24
                                   2-92

THE UNITED STATES

THE UNITED STATES

By the Editors of Time-Life Books
With photographs by Winnie Denker

TIME-LIFE BOOKS   ○   ALEXANDRIA, VIRGINIA

Other Publications:

UNDERSTANDING COMPUTERS
YOUR HOME
THE ENCHANTED WORLD
THE KODAK LIBRARY OF
   CREATIVE PHOTOGRAPHY
GREAT MEALS IN MINUTES
THE CIVIL WAR
PLANET EARTH
COLLECTOR'S LIBRARY OF THE CIVIL WAR
THE EPIC OF FLIGHT
THE GOOD COOK
WORLD WAR II
HOME REPAIR AND IMPROVEMENT
THE OLD WEST

This volume is one in a series of books describing countries of the world — their natural resources, peoples, histories, economies and governments.

For information on and a full description of any of the Time-Life Books series listed above, please write:
Reader Information
Time-Life Books
541 North Fairbanks Court
Chicago, Illinois 60611

THE COVER: Silhouetted against a wide, still-glowing Western sky, a Kansas farmer stops his pickup truck at dusk to collect the day's mail from his roadside mailbox.
   On the opposite page is the United States' official emblem, or Great Seal, which in addition to the national bird, a bald eagle, includes the country's motto, *"E pluribus unum"* — "Out of the many, one."

FRONT AND BACK ENDPAPERS: A topographic map showing the major rivers, plains, mountain ranges and other natural features of the United States appears on the front endpaper; the back endpaper shows the states and other political divisions.

Time-Life Books Inc.
is a wholly owned subsidiary of

TIME INCORPORATED

FOUNDER: Henry R. Luce 1898-1967

Editor-in-Chief: Henry Anatole Grunwald
President: J. Richard Munro
Chairman of the Board: Ralph P. Davidson
Corporate Editor: Ray Cave
Group Vice President, Books: Reginald K. Brack Jr.
Vice President, Books: George Artandi

TIME-LIFE BOOKS INC.

EDITOR: George Constable
Executive Editor: George Daniels
Editorial General Manager: Neal Goff
Director of Design: Louis Klein
Director of Editorial Resources: Phyllis K. Wise
Editorial Board: Dale M. Brown, Roberta Conlan, Ellen Phillips, Donia Ann Steele, Rosalind Stubenberg, Kit van Tulleken, Henry Woodhead
Director of Research and Photography: John Conrad Weiser

PRESIDENT: Reginald K. Brack Jr.
Executive Vice Presidents: John M. Fahey Jr., Christopher T. Linen
Senior Vice President: James L. Mercer
Vice Presidents: Stephen L. Bair, Edward Brash, Ralph J. Cuomo, Juanita T. James, Wilhelm R. Saake, Robert H. Smith, Paul R. Stewart, Leopoldo Toralballa

LIBRARY OF NATIONS

SERIES DIRECTOR: Dale M. Brown
Designer: Thomas S. Huestis
Chief Researcher: Jane Edwin
Editorial Staff for *The United States*
Associate Editors: Jim Hicks, David S. Thomson (text); Jane Speicher Jordan (pictures)
Staff Writer: Roberta Conlan
Researchers: Elise Ritter-Gibson (principal), Denise Li, Rita Mullin, Paula York-Soderlund
Assistant Designer: Robert K. Herndon
Copy Coordinator: Margery duMond
Picture Coordinator: Linda Lee
Editorial Assistant: Myrna E. Traylor

Special Contributors: The chapter texts were written by: Ezra Bowen, Ron Bailey, Donald Dale Jackson, Richard Stengel, Bryce Walker, and Bernard Weisberger.

Other Contributors: LaVerle Berry, Rosemary George, Philip Payne and A.B.C. Whipple.

Editorial Operations
Copy Chief: Diane Ullius
Editorial Operations: Caroline A. Boubin (manager)
Production: Celia Beattie
Quality Control: James J. Cox (director)
Library: Louise D. Forstall

Correspondents: Elisabeth Kraemer-Singh (Bonn); Margot Hapgood, Dorothy Bacon (London); Maria Vincenza Aloisi, Josephine du Brusle (Paris); Ann Natanson (Rome). Valuable assistance was also provided by Carolyn Chubet and Christina Lieberman (New York).

Assistant Editor for the U.S. Edition: Karin Kinney

CONSULTANTS

Russel B. Nye, Distinguished Professor, Emeritus, at Michigan State University, is the author of dozens of books and articles about United States history and culture, including a Pulitzer Prize-winning biography of 19th-century historian George Bancroft.

William A. Cox is the Congressional Research Service's Senior Specialist for Economic Policy. A former Deputy Chief Economist of the U.S. Department of Commerce, he has written numerous articles on the American economy.

PHOTOGRAPHER

Danish-born photographer Winnie Denker has traveled the world for more than 10 years, taking pictures for such diverse publications as *Paris-Match, Marie-Claire* and *Parents* magazines. She has worked in Bali, Samoa, India and Egypt. She spent more than two months touring the United States for this volume in the Library of Nations series.

First printing.
Published simultaneously in Canada.
School and library distribution by Silver Burdett Company, Morristown, New Jersey.

TIME-LIFE is a trademark of Time Incorporated U.S.A.

Library of Congress Cataloguing in Publication Data
Main entry under title:
The United States.
   (Library of Nations)
   Bibliography: p.
   Includes index.
   1. United States.   I. Time-Life Books.
II. Series: Library of Nations (Alexandria, Va.)
E156.U54 1986   973   86-1469
ISBN 0-8094-5112-3
ISBN 0-8094-5303-7 (lib. bdg.)

CONTENTS

Rimmed by docks and bridges, New York's Manhattan Island glimmers in the early-morning light. The round fort at its southern tip *(bottom, center left)*

6

served as a processing center for immigrants entering the United States from Europe before facilities on nearby Ellis Island were built.

A BURGEONING OF SERVICES

As early as 1950, the productivity of U.S. farms and factories allowed more than 50 percent of the work force to labor in service industries — a category including everything from medical care to fast-food operations. Three decades later an enormous 67 percent of all workers were in services, while increased mechanization cut the number of farm workers to scarcely 3.6 percent of the total and industrial workers to 29.3 percent.

AGRICULTURE
INDUSTRY
SERVICES

65
60
55
50
45
40
35
30
25
20
15
10
5
%

1950   1980

A specialized part of the huge U.S. service industry, a 7-Eleven grocery purveys snacks, staples and other goods to customers in Dallas, Texas. Once open from

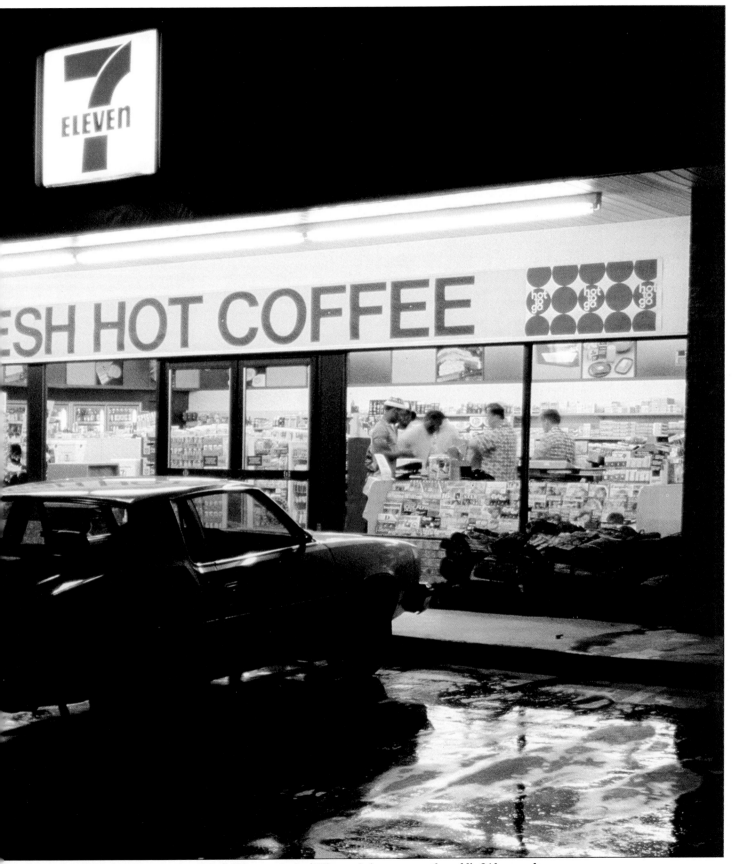

a.m. to 11 p.m. — thus the name — most of the 7,000 stores in the 7-Eleven chain now serve the public 24 hours a day.

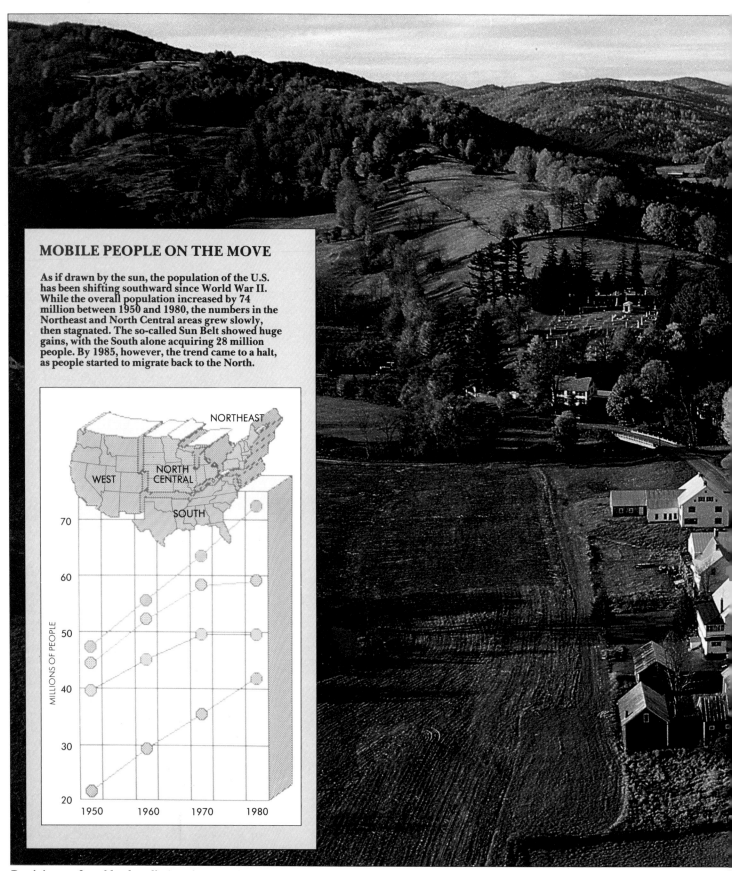

MOBILE PEOPLE ON THE MOVE

As if drawn by the sun, the population of the U.S. has been shifting southward since World War II. While the overall population increased by 74 million between 1950 and 1980, the numbers in the Northeast and North Central areas grew slowly, then stagnated. The so-called Sun Belt showed huge gains, with the South alone acquiring 28 million people. By 1985, however, the trend came to a halt, as people started to migrate back to the North.

NORTHEAST

NORTH CENTRAL

WEST

SOUTH

MILLIONS OF PEOPLE

70

60

50

40

30

20

1950   1960   1970   1980

Reminiscent of an older, bucolic America, the village of Strafford, Vermont, settled in 1761, nestles amid rolling hills and trees flamed by autumn.

Vermont remains the least urban of all 50 states; 66.2 percent of its people live as their ancestors did, on farms and in small towns.

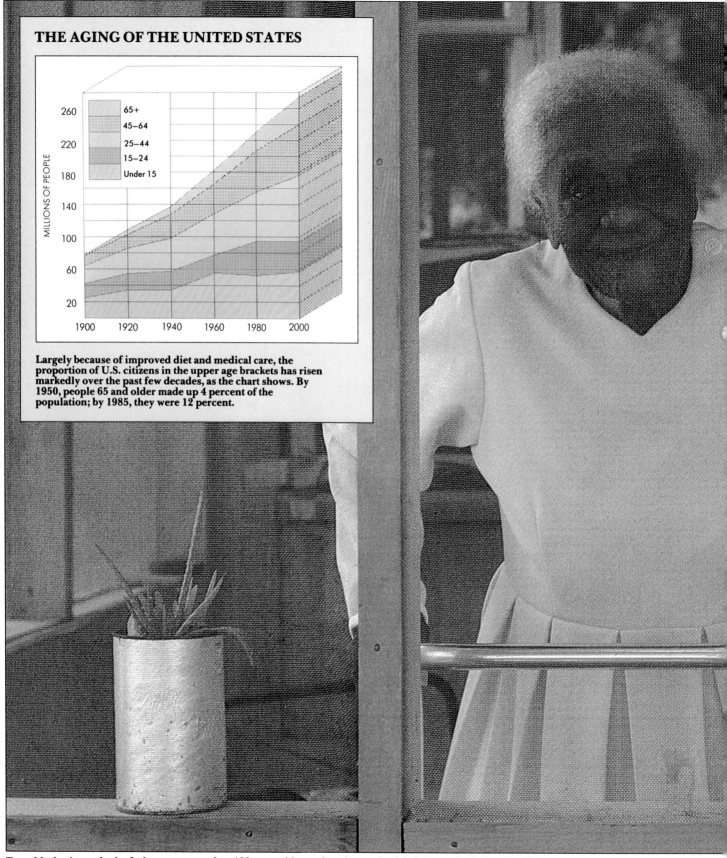

THE AGING OF THE UNITED STATES

MILLIONS OF PEOPLE

- 65+
- 45–64
- 25–44
- 15–24
- Under 15

260
220
180
140
100
60
20

1900 1920 1940 1960 1980 2000

Largely because of improved diet and medical care, the proportion of U.S. citizens in the upper age brackets has risen markedly over the past few decades, as the chart shows. By 1950, people 65 and older made up 4 percent of the population; by 1985, they were 12 percent.

Two elderly sisters, both of whom are more than 100 years old, stand on the porch of their house in the hamlet of Two Egg, Florida.

A section of the 800-mile-long trans-Alaskan pipeline snakes through a pass in the Brooks Range, not far from its beginning in the oilfields around

PRODIGAL PRODUCER OF ENERGY

Consuming more energy than any other nation, the United States is also among the world leaders in energy production. The statistics for the mid-1980s, charted in the graph at right, show the U.S. in first place in the output of hydroelectricity, but in second place in the production of coal, oil and natural gas.

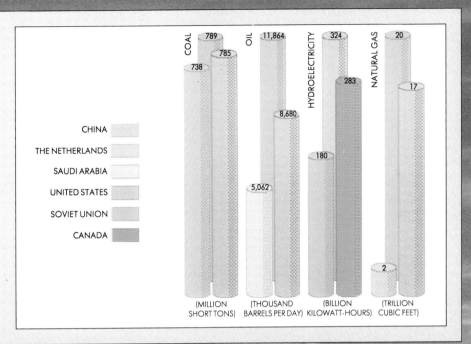

CHINA
THE NETHERLANDS
SAUDI ARABIA
UNITED STATES
SOVIET UNION
CANADA

COAL 789 785 738 (MILLION SHORT TONS)

OIL 11,864 8,680 5,062 (THOUSAND BARRELS PER DAY)

HYDROELECTRICITY 324 283 180 (BILLION KILOWATT-HOURS)

NATURAL GAS 20 17 2 (TRILLION CUBIC FEET)

Prudhoe Bay. The lights of Pump Station No. 4, which helps boost the oil on its journey, twinkle in the distance.

"Give me your tired, your poor / Your huddled masses yearning to breathe free," run the lines on the base of the Statue of Liberty. Though written a century ago, they are as meaningful today as then. Indeed, they contain one of the core truths about the United States: that it is a nation built by people who came from somewhere else, almost all with the same purpose—to better themselves.

The freedom the immigrants sought and found was not just political and religious; it was social. They were released from the class restraints of the Old World. A poor English weaver, who had emigrated in 1830 to New York State, wrote in a letter home to his wife: "America is not like England, for here no man thinks himself your superior. An American, however low his station, never feels himself abashed when entering the presence of the highest. This is a country where a man can stand as a man, and where he can enjoy the fruits of his own exertions, with rational liberty to the fullest extent." (A glaring exception to this cheerful situation was America's population of black slaves; but in time, their fight for freedom and liberty would reconfirm the nation's ideals.)

Continually revitalized by fresh infusions of immigrants, America could draw on the rich personal resources of all the newcomers to challenge a succession of frontiers. First there was *the* frontier, the one that demarcated the extent of pioneer settlement of the American wilderness. Land-seeking European immigrants pouring in through Atlantic ports pushed this frontier farther and farther west—and its movement was greatly accelerated by the work of other immigrants, from China, who helped build the railroads that carried many settlers to the new territory.

In little more than a century the population of the U.S. increased by almost 20 times, from 3.9 million in 1790 to 75.9 million in 1900. This frontier era was marked by violence; the settlers almost exterminated the Indians, grabbing their land and destroying their cultures and means of existence. But it was also a time of courage and promise that gave rise to the enduring Old West ideals and myths—perhaps most notably that of the lone hero who secures justice with a fast gun—that thereafter pervaded both the foreigner's view of America and America's idea of itself.

In 1890, the U.S. Bureau of the Census formally declared that the frontier had ceased to exist. The West was not literally filled up with settlers, of course, but there was no longer a recognizable line west of which lived fewer than two persons per square mile—the Census Bureau's definition of the frontier. Yet the inflow of people did not abate; in fact, it increased. In six of the years between 1905 and 1914, immigration exceeded a million people annually, the highest yearly totals ever. Most came from Southern and Eastern European

INTRODUCTION

countries, and they helped populate a new American frontier of expanding cities and burgeoning industries.

In the 1920s Congress severely limited the number of foreigners who could move to the U.S. But in the reduced stream of immigrants were a significant number of intellectuals fleeing the spread of Fascism and anti-Semitism in Europe. These newcomers played crucial roles in the American exploration of yet another frontier, that of science. Among them was the German-born theoretical physicist Albert Einstein, one of the greatest scientific minds in history. They also included Enrico Fermi from Italy, who created the first nuclear chain reaction, and Hungarian-born Edward Teller, who was instrumental in the development of the hydrogen bomb.

Beginning in the late 1950s, the U.S. turned a substantial portion of its national energies — and wealth — to the exploration of perhaps the most exciting frontier of all: space. The space program, which involves danger (ten astronauts were killed in spacecraft accidents),

Papers in hand, a mother waits anxiously with her daughter on Ellis Island in the early part of the 20th century. The immigration processing center, located in New York harbor, was in operation from 1892 until 1943, when World War II stemmed the flow of aliens from abroad.

intense competition (national honor was at stake in a race with the Soviet Union) and a dream (putting men on the moon, finally fulfilled in 1969), has become the new archetypal American adventure. But in space, too, the tradition of the immigrant's role in American achievement has held true: One of the people who helped make space travel possible was Wernher von Braun, a German rocket engineer who became a U.S. citizen in 1955.

As the frontier of space expands, still other frontiers are evolving. The latest is that of high technology, and it is outmoding many of the old, heavy "smokestack" industries and hurting cities in which they once flourished. What will be the fate of the workers who are now losing jobs to automation? And what of the cities? Can they be revived? The answers may not be clear for decades. In the meantime, the country has opened its gates to another wave of immigrants, mostly from Southeast Asia and Latin America. Perhaps they can solve some of today's problems. If so, these new Americans will be reconfirming the nation's faith that each successive immigrant group is, as one American has so eloquently stated it, "the bearer of some mental or spiritual gift which is unique, and which we cannot afford to lose."

Seattle's huge domed stadium, the
Kingdome, seating 75,000 baseball or
football fans, echoes the shape of
Washington State's more famous
landmark, Mount Rainier. The
highest peak in the Cascade Range at
14,410 feet, it appears to loom over
Seattle although it is 100 miles away.

LAND OF NEW BEGINNINGS

In a movie house in East Africa not long ago, a scene in a Hollywood film prompted a woman to remark caustically, "That's America for you." The screen, as she spoke, was ablaze with the neon glare of Las Vegas, Nevada, one of America's Western gambling meccas. The woman's comment suggested that the whole United States was like this — a gaudy concoction of tasteless commercialism.

Moments later the film contradicted her when the scene shifted to the austere expanse of adjacent desert, then upward nearly 12,000 feet to the peaks of nearby mountains, whose snow formed a silver-white mantle to outdazzle the brightest boomtown neon. At this, a British journalist seated behind the woman said aloud, "In one sweep of the eye we've seen the likes of the Serengeti Plains and the Alps as well. It's a wonder any American ever bothers to go abroad."

A wonder, indeed. For America embraces such a varied richness of terrain, such a range of environment, such an extraordinary breadth both of physical resource and of vista that it has been a kind of promised land from the very beginning. About 240 million people now live in the United States, and all of them or their ancestors — including the Asian forebears of the American Indians themselves — came to America from somewhere else.

To a newcomer, perhaps the most striking feature of the country is its size: 3.5 million square miles, making the United States the fourth largest nation in the world (after the Soviet Union, Canada and China). The distance between Boston and San Francisco is greater than the distance between Paris and Baghdad.

America's vastness has been crucial both in luring people from abroad and in shaping American attitudes and aspirations. From atop a tractor on the table-flat Great Plains, nothing stops the eye through the full, 360-degree sweep of the compass; the world seems to consist of sky and sun and wheat and wind. With few, if any, limits upon one's outer vision, it is unnatural for the inner eye to perceive many limits on what a person can say or do, or how he or she may choose to live or worship.

Americans built their country in this spirit: The First Amendment of the Constitution says, with a clarity that two centuries have not much muddied, "Congress shall make no law respecting an establishment of religion, or prohibiting the free exercise thereof; or abridging the freedom of speech." From atop such principles, a human being can see forever.

Today, after some 200 years of urbanization, the sense and reality of space still exist all over the United States. Towns and cities holding more than three fourths of the country's population take up only 2 percent of the land in the 48 contiguous states. Author Gertrude Stein summed up this

1

enduring elbow room succinctly: "In the United States," she wrote, "there is more land where nobody is than where anybody is."

However, the strength and wonder of the United States lie in the land's diversity rather than its extent. Back from the Atlantic Coast rises a lush country of forests and mountains and grassy plains, drained by a lacework of rivers — including the Mississippi-Missouri-Ohio river system, the longest in the world — and crowned by the five connected Great Lakes. In the West, spectacular crags with glaciered flanks climb to nearly 15,000 feet, and Alaska's Mount McKinley tops 20,000 feet, higher than the highest of the Alps. Within 100 miles of California's Mount Whitney — at 14,495 feet the highest point in the contiguous 48 states — the ground drops to 280 feet below sea level in the small, roasting desert called Death Valley.

Yet extremes of geography and climate are by no means the dominant features of American life. America's diversity, while striking, is manageable. Most of the country lies in the temperate zone. There are no sweltering jungles; the nearest equivalents are small patches of mangrove swamp in Florida and Louisiana. The Soviet Union and Canada have enormous reaches of arctic tundra that are all but uninhabitable, but more than four fifths of the United States is usable, even comfortable, space. This land of manageable diversity is a natural place for things to grow and to flourish.

And flourish they do. Noah could still collect a tremendous variety of wild beasts from the land and its adjacent waters: grizzly bears and whales, alligators and giant California condors, gray wolves and antelope. And there is a similarly rich endowment of wild plants, including both the biggest and the oldest living things on earth: the Pacific Coast's sequoia trees, some of which tower more than 380 feet and measure 30 feet through the trunk, and bristlecone pines that sprouted nearly 5,000 years ago.

In the great Mississippi-Missouri-Ohio drainage basin, the soil is so rich and dark that the poet Robert Frost described it as "good enough to eat." Good enough, at any rate, that the three states of Kansas, Nebraska and Minnesota alone produce enough meat and grain to provide a meal a day for every soul in the U.S. and Canada throughout the year — with some left over for Mexico.

"Land is a given," wrote educator

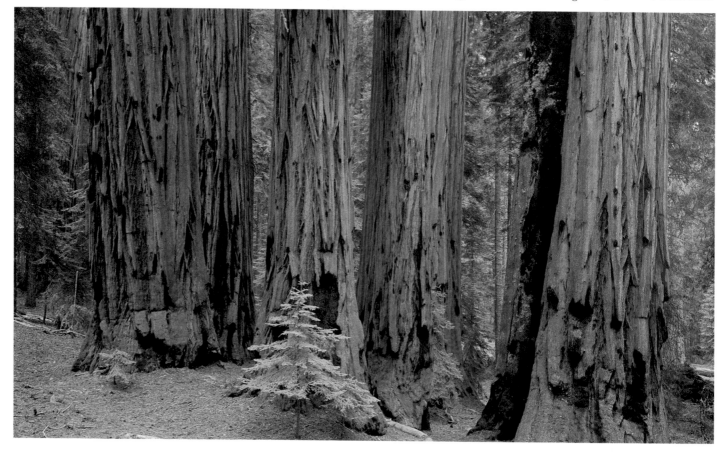

Theodore M. Hesburgh. "It may be well or badly used. It is only the spirit and character of a people that eventually shape a land, forge a nation upon it." Americans have shaped some of their land with a vengeance — and with mixed results.

The American Indians had a reverent attitude toward the land, considering it fundamentally unpossessable, but the people who arrived from other shores had no such compunctions. They regarded the land as something for them to master. To tap the riches that lay beneath its surface, they sank shafts deep into the earth to bring up the minerals, or they simply stripped off the surface — despoiling the vegetation in the process — to get at the veins of coal lying just beneath.

More admirably, the newcomers have managed to transform uninhabitable deserts into lush garden spots. California's huge Imperial Valley once was a desiccated place to be gotten across as quickly as possible. But since 1940, when the All-American Canal — part of the federal irrigation system that also includes the Hoover Dam — was completed, water has gushed into the dry soil of the valley, producing an abundance of lettuce, carrots, melons and tomatoes.

The urge to tame and fill the country's spaces has occasionally operated with astonishing speed. Could any other people, to choose one perfectly American example, have staged the Oklahoma land rush? On a wonderfully absurd morning in 1893, the U.S. government opened to settlement the last official tract of Indian Territory, 10,000 square miles of good grazing land known as the Cherokee Outlet. At noon on September 16, 100,000 land-hungry pioneers lined up at the Out-

let's edge aboard wagons, on horses, afoot and even on bicycles, all of them intent on staking out a share of the land. A gun went off, and away they went in a cloud of dust. It was the essence of opportunism, a great game open to all, with the prime acres going to the swiftest.

The diversity of all those who came to America has at times proved less manageable than the diversity of the land itself. The African slaves and their descendants had to struggle for centuries to achieve even their present imperfect equality with white Americans — many of whose ancestors arrived long after the blacks did. Gang fights between different ethnic and racial groups have been a recurring feature in some American cities. Still, immigrants generally have been assimilated within a generation or two, as each new group got a foothold on the ladder to economic success.

Television, radio, newspapers and magazines have helped in this process of integration by instilling a common value system. The United States contains some 150 million television sets. There are two radios for every human being in the nation. Each morning some 1,700 daily papers hit the street; the total circulation of all periodicals tops 210 million.

Another great tie binding the country together is transportation. Americans own about 167 million automobiles, which travel 1.7 trillion passenger miles each year. Moreover, they fly 243 billion annual airline passenger miles. Today's Americans — those who can afford to, at any rate — can travel anywhere they desire, learning about the various regions of the country as they go.

Critics contend that such mobility

and the pervasive influence of radio and television, while helping to unify the United States, have also homogenized the country's culture. It is certainly true that chain business establishments — McDonald's hamburgers, Holiday Inn motels, Kentucky Fried Chicken — have tended to standardize eating habits and travelers' accommodations. Thousands of near-identical shopping malls — commercial villages with all amenities at hand — dot the suburbs. And the sounds of Muzak — the trade name for piped-in music tailored to stimulate people to buy more or to work more efficiently — are heard across the land.

As New Brunswick, New Jersey, Omaha, Nebraska, and Chula Vista, California, take to such standardization, the country's old multiplicity of local cuisines and life styles, as well as attitudes and even regional accents, may be vanishing. "The divisions of America — North, South, East, West — have long been blurred," wrote author Lillian Hellman. "We have moved too much, intermarried with too many other split levels, cars and freezers to leave behind anything more than pockets of the past."

Perhaps so. But if a traveler from abroad were to tour the U.S., stopping to watch and listen and think, he or she would find some surprises in the size, the spirit and the significance of these pockets. The traveler might conclude that America is not so much growing bland as simply growing up, at a cost of some youthful charm but with many of its personal and regional distinctions still intact.

The tour might begin in New England, the six states of Maine, New Hampshire, Vermont, Massachusetts, Connecticut and Rhode Island. All ex-

Deeply furrowed bark indicates the great age — up to 3,000 years — of California's giant sequoias. About 5,000 of these huge trees, the world's largest, stand safe from the logger's ax in the 386,863-acre Sequoia National Park, in the Sierra Nevada.

1

Scores of pleasure craft crowd the
protected harbor of Marblehead, Massachusetts, one of New England's
oldest fishing ports. Founded in 1633,
it is now a choice suburb of Boston.

cept landlocked Vermont share a portion of the crinkled Atlantic coastline, where cozy harbors still shelter New England's commercial fishing fleet. Today, many New Englanders sail simply for fun: On a summer weekend, thousands of pleasure craft speckle the waters of Long Island Sound, Vineyard Sound and Buzzards Bay. But their seagoing ancestors, fishing for cod or pursuing whales around the globe, brought the region its first prosperity.

Away from the sea, the wooded mountains cradle, here and there, a white-spired church or a patchwork of fields where cows still crop the grass right up to the stone walls. The strongest vestiges of traditional Yankee character survive in northern New England — an area long inhabited by close-mouthed country people, crafty in a deal, hard-working, thrifty, conservative about family and religion but sometimes radical in politics, proud, dry-witted and hard to push around.

Perhaps the best-known exemplar of New England taciturnity was the nation's 30th president, Calvin Coolidge, or "Silent Cal." Anecdotes about the man are worn as smooth as river rocks. On one occasion Coolidge was presented with a garden rake by an orator who said that the implement was made of hickory wood. The orator then long-windedly compared the resiliency of hickory to the character of the new president from Vermont. Coolidge studied the rake for a long time and said, "Ash." On a train trip with the president, a companion, made restless by Coolidge's habitual silence, pointed out the window at a field full of sheep and noted, "The sheep have been sheared." Coolidge's cool reply: "Looks like it from this side."

The true Yankee is honest heir to the values of New England's founding Puritans, with their high regard for work, church, community and righteousness. Today many of those values survive, though the New Englanders have changed, as has much of the countryside. It is hard to find an outward trace of the old Yankee in some parts of the highly urbanized southern New England state of Connecticut, at least in the heavily Italian industrial crush of Bridgeport or New Haven or among the clerks of giant insurance companies in Hartford. Many of the strong-handed families who farm the Connecticut Valley, the major agricultural area of New England, have ways analogous to those of the Yankee, but their roots are in Poland.

Not even Boston, queen city of New England, retains much that is purely Yankee, except for a patrician cadre referred to as the Brahmins. These are the long-established moneyed families who once ran the city and exerted great influence, but who have been generally upstaged in the political arena by Boston's shrewd Irish politicians — the Curleys, McCormicks, Fitzgeralds, O'Neills and Kennedys.

On the whole, Boston is a mix of communities, with sizable Irish, Italian, Afro-American and Puerto Rican populations. Many of these have ancestors who came to the city to work in the leather-goods and textile mills, foundries and firearms factories that once made New England the leader in U.S. manufacturing. Much of that industry is gone now.

The region has moved instead into the business world of high-technology electronics — with great success, particularly in and around Boston. This new field has sprung from a magnificent seedbed of colleges and universi-

23

1

ties — among them some of the world's finest, such as Harvard University and the Massachusetts Institute of Technology — that have been collecting in the area since before the United States came into existence. In the Boston area alone flourish more than 60 degree-granting institutions.

Despite new industries and new people, there lingers in New England an adherence to old ways — and a stiff-backed contrariness about being told what to do. "Live free or die" is the motto stamped on New Hampshire license plates — produced, ironically, by the state's prison inmates. And not long ago, in a bit of Yankee revivalism, a New Hampshire town named Walpole took the risk of economic demise by voting down a proposal to permit construction of a pulp mill, whose new jobs would have come at the perceived price of giving the town over to the mill.

Such individualism does not always mean rejecting something new. Not long ago, a town meeting in the Vermont hamlet of Craftsbury was considering whether to create a fire-fighting district within part of the town, so that the town could raise capital on its own to salvage an aging water facility. A voter who had recently moved to the area objected, claiming that the proposal would change the "character" of Craftsbury. At that point a trusted old-timer stood up to say, "I've lived in Craftsbury all my life, and as long as I'm here, it won't change." The vote ran three to one against the newcomer and for the fire district. "You have to learn to quiet up when you first move into a small town," explained one woman.

Below New England lies the Middle Atlantic seaboard, an area of wealth, power and tremendous ethnic diversity. Nowhere are these qualities more

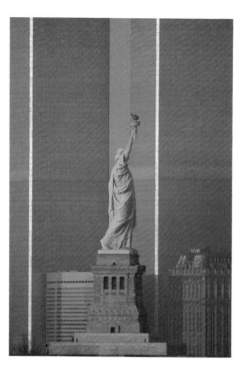

evident than in New York City, the region's dynamo.

This roaring urban monster, with more than nine million residents in its metropolitan area (packed 64,000 to the square mile in the city's heart, Manhattan) pulses out its messages of commerce and entertainment to the whole earth. The New York stock exchanges trade the majority of all corporate shares publicly bought and sold in the United States; six of the nation's 10 biggest banks are based here; and the headquarters buildings of the nation's three predominant television networks — American Broadcasting Companies (ABC), Columbia Broadcasting System (CBS) and National Broadcasting Company (NBC) — tower within blocks of one another.

New York lures people from everywhere: Some 17.5 million tourists arrive annually, more than visit any other American city, and gape upward at the soaring skyscrapers. It long attracted, as the country's principal port of entry, millions of immigrants, with the result that it became the most ethni-

cally mixed of all the cities in the United States.

Ukrainian-born taxi drivers joke with each other in the accents of the Dnieper basin over their radios. The Central Park Mall hosts Italian opera in Korean. On Sixth Avenue, a streetside West Indian steel-drum band plunks away for handouts. A Puerto Rican market flourishes in Spanish Harlem. Exuberant conversations in Greek are heard in coffeehouses in the section called Astoria, while teen-age gangs war tong-style in Manhattan's Chinatown. Up in Harlem and elsewhere in slums with boarded-up and burned-out buildings, the city's black population struggles to break out of its cycle of low opportunity and low income, while all over town the biggest urban concentration of Jews on earth — almost six times the number of citizens residing in Israel's twin cities of Tel Aviv-Jaffa — energizes the professions, commerce and the arts.

The atmosphere changes south of New York. The pace of life in Philadelphia, Pennsylvania, and Baltimore, Maryland, and their hinterlands is noticeably slower than in the larger metropolis to the north. And among the very rich who preside over the quiet elegance of estates along the Chesapeake Bay's shores and around Philadelphia there is an insistence upon understatement. A Philadelphia dowager who is directly descended from a signer of the Declaration of Independence — and whose 32 grandchildren have each received from her a gift of more than $500,000 — runs her own errands in a modest two-door sedan.

The climate, too, is softer here, the fields more fecund and more manicured, the hills lower, the river estuaries braided with marshes full of game fish and water birds. Perhaps the only time of noisy tension in rural Pennsylvania is mid-autumn, when thousands of deer hunters shoot up the woods with such a free hand that one old-timer pronounced himself "safer in the second battle of the Marne" than on a deer hunt outside the state capital of Harrisburg.

To the south is Washington, D.C., a federal enclave of tree-lined boulevards, imposing marble buildings and sidewalk drug dealers, of revered national monuments and boldly importuning prostitutes.

Washington employs 346,000 federal civilian workers and keeps many tens of thousands of other people busy in government-serving enterprises. So many of the government's activities in-

volve legal questions that the city can claim roughly one lawyer for every 50 inhabitants, the highest ratio in the nation. (Washington also has more psychiatrists per capita than any other U.S. city.) In addition, the city attracts crowds of consultants and journalists as well as lobbyists, people who make a career of trying to influence the government on behalf of corporations or special-interest groups.

A majority of these lawyers, consultants and others who cluster around the government are white and relatively well-off, and many of them live in the suburbs of nearby Maryland or Virginia. The population of Washington itself is 70 percent black and suffers from chronic unemployment.

West of the Middle Atlantic seaboard

is the Great Lakes region, an area dedicated to production — in its enormous factories and clashing foundries. But the steelmakers and other manufacturers fell on hard times during the late 1970s and early 1980s, as foreign competition and worldwide economic recession cut deeply into their markets.

Shutdowns among the old, so-called smokestack industries of cities from Youngstown, Ohio, to Gary, Indiana, reversed a decades-long influx of job-seekers into the region. Some unemployed workers loaded their families and belongings into their cars and set off to search for jobs in the new high-technology and service industries of the South and Southwest.

Still, America remains the world's third-largest steel producer and the world's leading manufacturer of automobiles. And the economy of the Midwest, which includes the farming states of the central plains as well as the Great Lakes states, has a robust agricultural base. Although the recession of 1981 and 1982 still threatens the survival of some seven to 15 percent of family farms, the long view is one of continued prosperity for the region.

The state of Iowa has built upon its farming wealth a cultural edifice that includes a renowned symphony orchestra at Des Moines and a highly regarded writers' workshop at the University of Iowa. At an Iowa agricultural research center, beneath a mural by Grant Wood, one of the country's great painters, is the motto, "When tillage begins, other arts follow." Apparently so. In the twin cities of Minneapolis-St. Paul, Minnesota, long America's flour-milling center, more than a million tickets a year are sold for theater, symphony and dance events.

In the heart of this vast region flourishes the metropolis many people regard as the epitome of the nation's way of life: Chicago, Illinois. Poet Carl Sandburg described it as the "City of the Big Shoulders . . . Tool Maker, Stacker of Wheat, Player with Railroads and the Nation's Freight Handler. . . ." The location of Chicago was hardly inviting in the beginning — a boggy, insect-infested piece of real estate on the shore of Lake Michigan. But the work-minded pioneers who first settled there did not care.

Chicago today is America's leader in the production of steel, communications equipment, industrial machinery, household appliances and musical instruments. The city has three of the world's five tallest buildings, including the tallest, the Sears Tower. Chicago also boasts O'Hare Airport, one of the busiest on earth, which sends some 50 million passengers a year to more than 230 direct destinations. Only 11 nations in the world generate more services and goods than Chicago.

For all the bustle and change, the Midwest hangs on to its hometown ways. Like the prairie itself, the people tend to be more open and outgoing than those back East. Iowa towns still hold quilting bees. Any autumn Saturday afternoon, half the town of Lincoln, Nebraska, cheers the local football heroes, and on winter weekend nights, it seems all of Indiana is at a basketball game.

The people are also self-possessed. One day Kansas City steak-house proprietor Arthur Bryant looked out from his modest establishment to behold an arriving flotilla of police and Secret Service cars — and the presidential limousine. Out stepped then-chief executive Jimmy Carter, hungry for some good Kansas City beef. Betraying not even the slightest awe, Bryant greeted Carter with a line from an old popular song. "If I'd known you were coming," he joked, "I'd have baked a cake."

Below the Midwest and the Middle Atlantic seaboard is the South, the old Confederate States of America whose secession from the rest of the United States led to the Civil War in the 1860s. Southerners still frequently refer to their region by its old nickname, Dixie, and cherish their neighborly, mannerly, easy-does-it, God-fearing traditions.

Here young boys are taught to stand up when a woman or an older man enters a room, and a question gets a smile and an answer that ends in "Sir" or "Ma'am." It is a place where a Mississippi dirt farmer gets out of bed and into his pickup truck at 2 a.m. on a rainy

A jagged skyline of recently built skyscrapers bespeaks the vitality of Chicago, Illinois, the Midwest's biggest city. The showpiece is the pyramidal Hancock Tower, soaring 1,100 feet above Lakeshore Drive *(foreground)*.

1

night to carry a poor neighbor's sick child 50 miles to the nearest big hospital, then quietly pays the doctor himself, with the shy explanation later to the neighbor that there was no fee. Departing visitors, whether saying goodby after a week with relatives or simply pulling away from a gas pump, hear the unvarying "Y'all come back and see us—hear?" And the speaker means it.

Religion remains a strong force. The Southern Baptist Convention is the largest and wealthiest Protestant church group in the U.S. So strong is the hand of pleasure-denying fundamentalism that Moore County, Tennessee, where craftsmen lovingly distill Jack Daniel's sour mash whiskey, forbids the sale of alcoholic spirits within its own borders.

Dixie remains defensive about its erstwhile prevalent attitudes toward the region's blacks, some 20 percent of the population; many of the schools remained racially segregated for years after the U.S. Supreme Court declared the practice to be unconstitutional in 1954. One consequence of segregation and other racist practices was a massive exodus of blacks from the region, particularly of younger blacks, that began in the 1920s and continued through most of the 1960s.

In recent years, however, the so-called "black problem" has gradually ceased to be an all-consuming issue. In 1981, Mississippi—which only 10 years earlier had the smallest number of registered black voters—led the nation in the number of elected black officials. Attitudes toward race, along with much else in the South, have undergone such change that the old Dixie lingers more as an idea, an emotion, than as a monolithic region.

The new South is richly productive.

It leads the nation in textile manufacturing, comes close in timber production and has gotten into such diverse industries as rubber and plastics, transportation equipment, petrochemicals and electrical parts. Cotton—once known as King Cotton to Southern farmers—has become but a consort to a newer, more valuable crop, soybeans.

High salaries paid to aerospace workers in Huntsville, Alabama, Houston, Texas, and Cape Canaveral, Florida, have helped narrow the wage gap between the South and the rest of the nation. New Orleans, once known principally for its French heritage, Dixieland jazz and uninhibited Mardi Gras festival, has overlaid the smell of gumbo (a local dish made with shellfish, okra, ham, chicken and sassafras, among other ingredients) with that of oil from offshore drilling rigs in the Gulf of Mexico. Petroleum-tanker traffic has turned this old city into the nation's busiest port.

Perhaps the most surprising aspect of all the change is the composition of the South's population. Lately, many more blacks—most of them young and well educated—have been moving back to the region than have been leaving it. Like hundreds of thousands of South-bound whites, they have been fleeing the high unemployment, high urban crime rate, pollution and cold winters of the North. Once again Dixie, now perhaps more widely known as the eastern arm of the Sun Belt, can proudly claim to be the land of good living.

Texas was part of the Confederacy, and the state's people still sing the South's Civil War song, "Dixie." But they sing "The Eyes of Texas" with more fervor, for this state is a region in itself, at least in spirit. Texas is a big

COMEBACK OF AN INSTITUTION

Small-town America is sometimes described in elegiac terms—as a comfortable way of life overtaken by the present and about to vanish forever. In truth, it is very much alive across much of the U.S., and even thriving. The latest census indicated that while the overall U.S. population grew by 4.8 percent in the last decade, towns of fewer than 2,500 inhabitants gained by 8.7 percent and those of 2,500 to 25,000 by 7.5 percent.

This rural resurgence is the result of several factors. More retirees with fixed incomes and the freedom to leave the high-priced cities and suburbs have fled to the country. Workers have followed their jobs into small towns as industries move out of inner cities and into more remote areas, often in the Sun Belt. Other Americans, tired of the hustle and bustle, the crime and grime of cities, have sought tranquillity in small towns everywhere.

One such refuge is Winterset, Iowa, population 4,000, located in rolling farmland 35 miles from Des Moines. Settled by Easterners in 1849, it still has six covered bridges, plus a town square (right), a volunteer fire department, 12 churches, three schools and nine small manufacturing plants, one hospital, three nursing homes, a weekly newspaper and scores of community groups devoted to everything from gardens to veterans' concerns. Since 1970, its population has grown by 10 percent.

Winterset, like many other U.S. small towns, may seem clannish, insular and dull to someone who needs a city's stimulation. But those who live there are compensated by a sense of belonging to a cohesive community that offers security and serenity—and a drugstore with a soda fountain.

Winterset's town square is bordered by 50 businesses, including a hair salon that offers California hairstyles. The square grows crowded on Saturday mornings, when farmers and townspeople come here to shop.

A big business as well as a diversion for people living in or near Winterset, Madison County's livestock auction takes place at least once a week. The signs on the wall advertise Winterset companies serving local farmers.

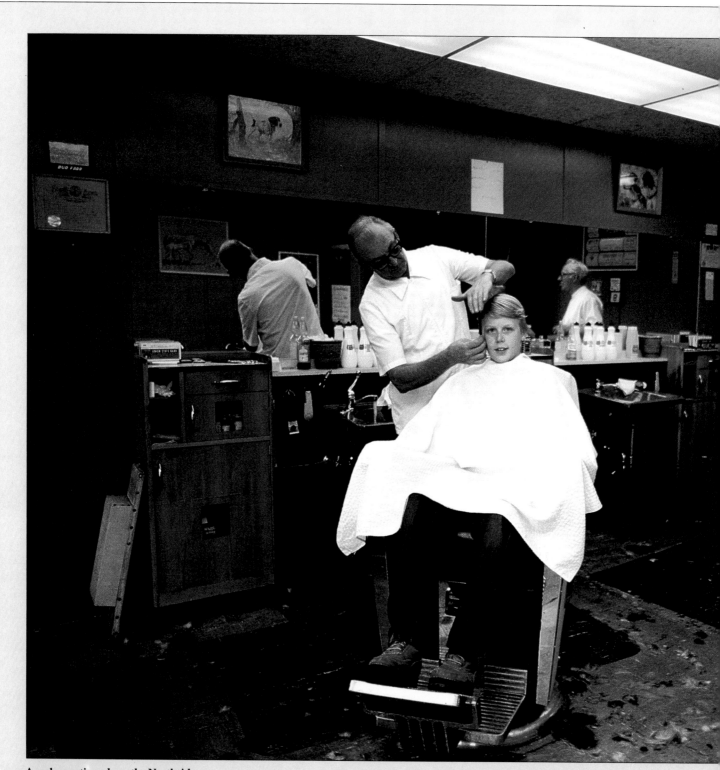

A male meeting place, the Northside
Barber Shop serves more than 100
customers, plus the "regulars" who
drop in for a daily chat.

A favorite gathering spot is the 100-year-old Montross Pharmacy, where citizens come for coffee breaks and the soda fountain's homemade pies and cinnamon rolls.

The birthplace of Winterset's most famous native son is now a museum. Marion Morrison — screen name: John Wayne — was born in this house on May 26, 1907. His father was one of the town druggists.

Erna Scherm plays the washboard for an elderly combo called the Hillbilly Band.

Marianne Fons *(left)* and Liz Porter work on a quilt. Winterset women's favorite activities are both old and new — quilting and aerobics.

Winterset's most peculiar recreation is horseback pool. Matt Porter *(left)* and other local rodeo riders will clump into a tavern for a game; their horses usually get nervous, however, and have to be tethered outside while the game is finished on foot.

A more popular sport in the town is basketball; here the high school's Huskies take a break while the crowd responds to the cheerleaders, including the team's mascot, seven-year-old Angela Bass *(foreground)*.

place (its 266,807 square miles make it 25 percent bigger than France), and most of its 14 million residents are proud of its size, its wealth and its rough-and-tumble frontier history.

Other Americans have not been so sure about Texas' charms. To many, the state's climate and countryside long have represented a national nadir of parched soil, nasty winters (except along the coast) and worst of all, searingly hot and humid summers. Philip Sheridan, a Northern general in the Civil War, remarked, "If I owned Texas and all Hell, I would rent out Texas and live in Hell."

But Texans have never paid much attention to anything said by people from anywhere else. Unlike their self-effacing Dixie neighbors, Texans are not afflicted by modesty. The residents of Dallas, who call their city "Big D," like to point out that the airport they share with nearby Fort Worth covers about the same amount of ground as all of Manhattan. They feel that their city is the natural habitat of the perennially slick and successful professional football team, the Dallas Cowboys, and of the team's perennially gorgeous cheerleaders. They are also gratified that Big D is home ground for what is probably the world's most expensive department store, Neiman-Marcus. There, a wealthy customer can pick up anything from a high-collared $100,000 sable coat to an exercise cycle that comes complete with a television screen and passing-scenery videotape.

The Dallas-Fort Worth area's population of three million is rivaled in Texas only by that of a booming sister metropolis, Houston, whose population had mushroomed by the mid-1980s to 2.9 million. Houston, not far from the Gulf of Mexico, can be the hot and hu-

mid alternative to Hell that General Sheridan had in mind. But Houstonians, determined that they should make their city livable as well as rich, keep comfortably cool by paying an annual air conditioning bill of close to one billion dollars. Much of this money comes from the offshore oil-drilling rigs in the Gulf of Mexico, whose lights wink above the horizon in the coastal haze of muggy summer nights. As all Texans will tell you, these wells have helped make their state the nation's leading oil producer.

Today, more than 75 percent of Texans live in these and other cities. Yet Texas' heart remains divided between its high-powered urban centers and its wide-open spaces. Despite all the braggadocio about big and new, so "down home," or countrified, does Texas profess to remain that its state legislature officially confers the winner's title at the world championship chili-cooking contest staged annually in the little southwest Texas town of Terlingua. And so proud are Texans of their cowboy heritage that big-city youths who have never been on horseback commonly wear high-heeled boots and broad-brimmed Stetson hats and ride mechanical bucking bulls in bars they call honky-tonks. All Texas schoolchildren learn early that their state was once (from 1836 to 1845) an independent republic.

A good deal of the state remains, indeed, not unlike the frontier of old. Outside the bounds of Houston's glitter and Dallas' moneyed urbanity, on the other side of a longitudinal boundary called the 100th meridian, lies a much simpler Texas of large ranches and small, dusty towns. This Texas belongs to the seemingly endless, empty spaces of the great West. Beyond the 100th

1

meridian the annual rainfall dwindles to 20 inches or less. All the way up the nation, cultivation is relatively easy to the east of this line. But to its west stretches short-grass country, where a steer needs 10 acres of land or more to survive and where crops will not grow without irrigation from dams or wells, which have to go down 900 feet in places to reach water.

In this arid, 864,000-square-mile vastness that reaches from western Texas through Arizona and north to Montana — and is broken by the imposing spine of the Rocky Mountains — live fewer people than in the New York and Washington, D.C., metropolitan areas combined. Population density for the entire region is about 13 souls to the square mile — which means that, in a lot of places, you cannot see your closest neighbor's house.

Moody relics of the region's history still lie scattered about: crumbled adobe walls, rusted mine machinery, zigzag slashes of mountain road going nowhere. In the northern Rockies the grass-grown ruts of the 19th-century Oregon Trail are still visible, so deeply were they cut by pioneer wagons. Wild horses, bighorn sheep and antelope continue to inhabit the region's deserts, sagebrush plains and mountains. The place names evoke the past: Wolf Point, Cheyenne Wells, Mule Shoe and Broken Bow.

This huge territory never did seem very hospitable. In 1821 Major Stephen Long, who led an expedition into what he then named the Great American Desert, pronounced the land "almost wholly unfit for cultivation and of course, uninhabitable." Indeed, were it not for the determination and the genius of the people who came after, it would still be that. Dry in summer, the high plains of Montana can be so cold in the winter that during blizzards healthy Hereford cattle are likely to freeze to death where they stand. "It's a deceitful country, hard, mean, with floods and droughts and tornadoes," said one resident. "But look at it," he added. "God Almighty, it's so beautiful."

Farmers who settled the southern and central Great Plains adopted hardy Russian winter wheat, which can grow in the dry conditions of the region. In the northern section they planted spring wheat, which is ready for harvest before the advent of the area's early and severe winters. As a result, significant stretches of what was once wasteland are today portions of the world's breadbasket.

One of the most striking achievements was the transformation of the land around Utah's Great Salt Lake, which Indians avoided because of its saline sterility. Here, in the mid-19th century, the Mormons, members of an austere theocratic society, chose to settle where they would not be bothered by anyone, and to make something of nothing. Gouging canals and dams into the snow fields of the neighboring Wasatch Mountains and developing large-scale irrigation methods, the Mormons turned the Salt Lake flats into a thriving metropolitan area of almost a million people living amid broad swaths of greenery.

Lately the cities of this part of the West have experienced an exponential growth. One reason is the climate: The southern portion of the region lies in the same Sun Belt that encompasses Dixie and that has grown in population more rapidly than any other part of the country between 1960 and 1985. A second factor that has helped turn the old cow towns and Spanish mission centers such as Albuquerque, New Mexico, into modern metropolises has been the West's extraordinary mineral and energy reserves.

Another, paradoxical attraction of this essentially spartan environment has been recreation and leisure. Over the years the federal government has incorporated 73.7 million acres nationwide into the National Park System, and some of the largest and most spectacular parks of the United States are located in the West. The government, in fact, owns almost 50 percent of all the land west of the 100th meridian. Millions of tourists annually visit such spectacular national parks as Bryce Canyon, Grand Teton, Yellowstone and Grand Canyon, as well as hundreds of other, smaller preserves.

But for many Americans, another region is probably even more exciting — and surely more naturally alluring. That is the Pacific states, which include California, Oregon, Washington, Hawaii and gigantic Alaska. Here is America's own promised land, the region to which Americans themselves have emigrated.

Hawaii lies a third of the way across the Pacific Ocean. In some ways it is the paradise it advertises itself to be. Made up of volcanic islands and coral atolls, the state sits just within the balmy northern rim of the tropics. Down from the mountain peaks on all the islands tumbles a profusion of tropical vegetation — lush ferns, brilliant hibiscus and stately palms. The sandy beaches and rolling surf of Hawaii are legendary. Naturally, tourism is one of the state's biggest industries.

Given such endowments, it is a wonder that the islands have not long since been submerged by mass migrations

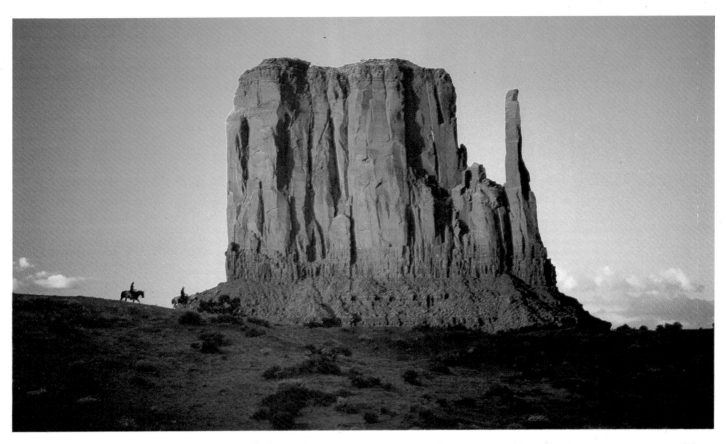

from mainland America. One deterrent is the lack of habitable space. So mountainous are the islands that the small, easternmost segments of Hawaii's 6,425-square-mile area contain almost all of the state's more than one million people.

Caucasians constitute about a third of the population. The islands' original Polynesian inhabitants, who were ravaged by diseases brought by missionaries, whalers and other early sojourners, today constitute less than 1 percent of all Hawaiians. The rest are a remarkable mix, mainly descendants of immigrants from Japan, the Philippines and China.

Hawaii has the nation's highest proportion of interracial marriages. The Caucasians tend to marry other Caucasians, and the Japanese still tend to marry other Japanese; for the remaining ethnic groups, however, more than half of all the marriages are made outside the group.

Both climate and opportunity — as well as the landscape — are wholly different in Alaska, which sprawls over an incredible 570,833 square miles; the United Kingdom, West Germany, France and Italy together could fit into it with space left over. Alaskan living is hard and winter temperatures can plunge to −60° F. There are few roads, and distances between settlements are so huge that most towns are supplied by sea or air. Fewer than half a million people have settled in this enormous space, 40 percent in and around the coastal city of Anchorage. For determined individuals, however, chances to make good abound.

Alaska holds the largest oil reserve in North America, near Prudhoe Bay on the Arctic coast. From there the oil is pumped through an 800-mile pipeline running south to the year-round ice-free port of Valdez. In the 1970s, a trucker or laborer working in the oilfields or along the pipeline earned an income equal to that of a successful New York executive. And although the cost of living is high in this air-lift economy, there is spare cash in Alaska — literally for everyone for as long as oil prices are soaring: In a period of several months in 1982 and 1983 when the value of oil peaked, the oil-glutted state gave a dividend of $1,000 to every adult state resident.

The people of the Pacific Northwest states — Washington and Oregon — flourish on quite another kind of bonus. Whereas much of Alaska is cold through most of the year, the relatively mild though moist climate of Washington and Oregon pervades a countryside that looks like a real-life replica of an idealized landscape painting. Within

1

sight of downtown Portland and Seattle rise snow-capped mountains. Lakes and protected bays have spawned hundreds of thousands of pleasure craft around Seattle alone.

The mighty Columbia River, forming some three fourths of the border between the two states, provides low-cost power for homes and industries. In the 1930s, the federal government began damming the river: The Grand Coulee, the Bonneville and 24 other dams in the system are the heart of a Northwest network that generates 43 percent of all the hydroelectric power in the nation.

Recent opinion surveys concluded

that Seattle and Portland are the two "most livable" cities in the United States. Seattle's location between Puget Sound and the Cascade Range makes it possible in summer for an outdoor enthusiast to sail, water-ski and even ski on the slopes close by — all in one exhilarating day.

With fewer available jobs to attract Americans compared to California to the south, the Northwest has not seen the influx of people that has made California the country's most populous state, home to 25 million people. California leads the nation in production of goods and services (were it an independent country, it would rank seventh in

the world in gross national product). But California also plays plenty.

This is the land of surfboards, hot tubs *(pages 40-41)* and Hollywood's Sunset Strip nightclubs. It was the birthplace of the 1960s hippie culture and, almost certainly, still is America's foremost consumer of illegal "recreational drugs," a fun-and-sun-loving state of endless golden beaches.

In California, wrote noted traveler and author John Gunther, "climate is worshipped as a god." But so too are money, fame, the perfection of the human body and the nebulous notions of self-awareness and self-fulfillment. Cultists and personality-enhancers

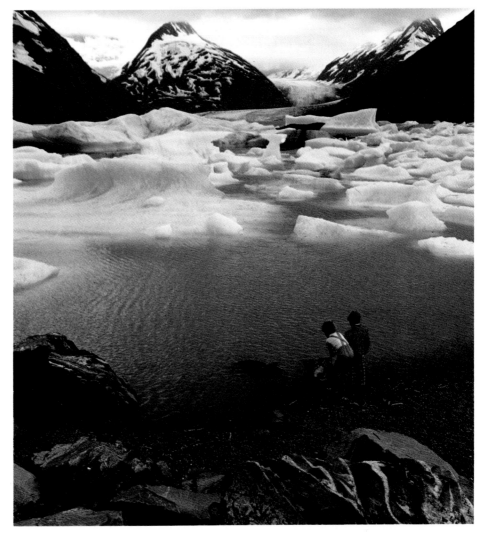

Children explore the crumbling edge of Portage Glacier, a river of ice that flows into Prince William Sound in south-central Alaska. The state has hundreds of glaciers, covering about 30 percent of the land.

promise lasting contentment through ever new schemes that are profitable for the originators, less effective for the subscribers.

California contains two of the most fascinating cities in the United States, San Francisco and Los Angeles (recognized throughout the world by its initials: L.A.). San Francisco may well be the country's best-loved city; many Americans list it on opinion polls as their favorite or at least as second-favorite, after their own hometowns. It may, indeed, be America's most beautiful. San Francisco gleams and sparkles atop a hilly peninsula between the Pacific Ocean and San Francisco Bay, and the city's most famous landmark, the glorious Golden Gate Bridge, soars across the narrows that divide the two bodies of water.

San Francisco is a city that never stops looking at itself, because its neighborhoods of boldly colored Victorian houses climb the sides and rise from the peaks of its 43 hills, offering countless stunning, irresistible views.

From San Francisco a highway winds 437 miles south to Los Angeles along one of the world's most breathtaking coastlines, where sheer cliffs drop into the pounding Pacific surf below. An inland route cuts through California's agricultural heart, the great Central Valley, one of the homes of the state's wine industry, its orchards and its huge agribusiness concerns. Here, too, are some remarkable sights: When tractors and harvesters switch on their headlights at dusk, they appear to be gigantic, glowing-eyed insects lumbering across the flat, fertile fields.

Newcomers driving to Los Angeles are never quite certain when they have reached the place. The municipal boundaries of the city encompass only

Off the shore of the Hawaiian island of Maui, a wind-surfer swoops down the face of a wave. Heavy Pacific swells make Hawaii a surfer's heaven. The native Polynesians were already enjoying the sport when the islands were discovered in 1778.

a small portion (464 square miles) of the metropolis generally known by the name of Los Angeles. Most of the urban complex lies within the 4,083 square miles of Los Angeles County, but many of the 11.5 million people who for all practical purposes are Angelenos actually reside in various parts of the four adjacent counties.

Built on an arid stretch of land, it is necessary for Los Angeles to import almost all of its water, some from as far as 250 miles away. From nature's standpoint, this may be the unlikeliest spot on earth for a great city to have been established, and nature at

times seems determined to prove it.

Probably no other urban center in the world is threatened by so many natural disasters. Waves driven by Pacific Ocean storms occasionally smash expensive houses built along the shores of Los Angeles' coastal communities, and mudslides caused by torrential rains frequently tumble other residences from their precarious hillside perches. Every few years forest fires fanned by hot, dry winds from the desert destroy millions of dollars' worth of homes. (What other city on earth is plagued by forest fires?)

Then there is the ever-present threat

A STATE WITH ITS OWN LIFESTYLE

"What we want the whole country to be," an ex-governor of California once said, "California already is." It leads the United States in farm income. It has the greatest concentration of high-technology industries in the world and is home to 30 percent of all the aeronautical engineers in the country; one Californian in 10 has a college degree. At the same time, the state is the center of antitechnology activities and prides itself on its strict ecological regulations. But most of all it is the trend setter for the American lifestyle.

California represents "absolute freedom, mobility, and privacy . . . the instinct which drove America to the Pacific," wrote California native and author Joan Didion. Of all the fads and movements that have influenced the country, more have arisen in California than in any other state.

From this benign climate came the ideal of the indoor-outdoor home — roof gardens, balconies, terraces, houseboats, patios and, more recently, hot tubs *(below)*. Here is the fountainhead of surfing, backpacking, all-day roller skating, the shopping center, sub-

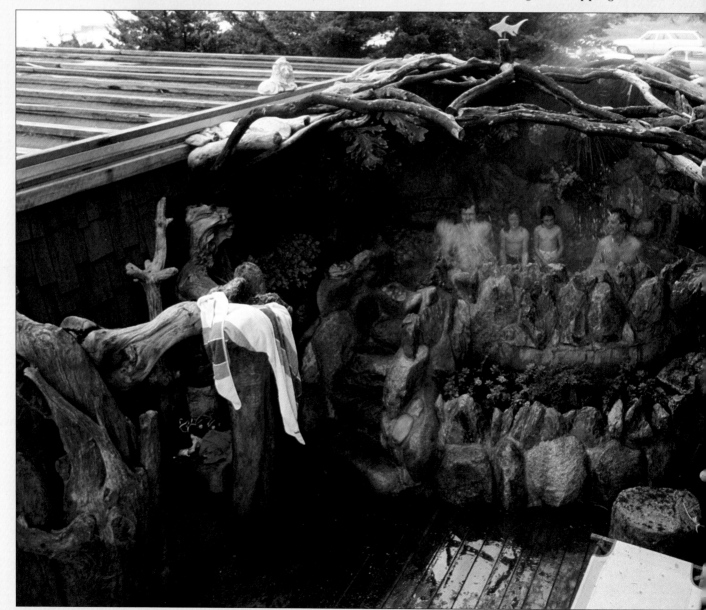

Photographer Michael Powers *(right)*, his daughter Marika and friends relax in Powers' hot tub — one of some 500,000 owned by Americans — near urban sprawl and life lived in the automobile: California has drive-in churches as well as drive-in supermarkets.

But California is not only a source of the new; it is also a goal. It is "the last stop," wrote Didion, "for all those who came from somewhere else, for all those who have drifted away from the cold and the past and the old ways."

he home he built south of San Francisco.

of earthquakes, which Los Angeles shares with San Francisco. Both lie perilously close to one of the earth's great geological rifts, the San Andreas Fault. Los Angeles suffers numerous earth tremors, including one not so long ago that brought down highway overpasses. Meanwhile, earthquake experts, as well as Angelenos and San Franciscans, await what they refer to as "the big one," a quake of cataclysmic proportions.

People and their automobiles do their share to increase the hazards and harassments of life in Los Angeles. There are an incredible 5.3 million motor vehicles registered in Los Angeles County alone, one for every 1.4 persons. Automobile exhaust fumes are the principal contributor to the city's notorious smog, a chemical haze that hangs suffocatingly over the Los Angeles basin most days, bringing tears to stinging eyes.

But Angelenos would not — indeed, could not — do without their cars. Los Angeles has sometimes been called a city in search of a center, because until fairly recently it lacked a definable downtown area. Now it has many "downtowns" scattered throughout the metropolis, each a concentration of high-rise commercial buildings. All four corners of Los Angeles County are linked together by 400 miles of conventional highways and expressways and 500 miles of superhighways called freeways — a glaring misnomer when standstill traffic jams snarl the system during rush hours. Public transportation is minimal: For all practical purposes, there is no other way to get around than by car.

Anyway, Angelenos love their automobiles. No amount of smog could stop movie moguls from swanning about in

their Rolls-Royces — although one distinctly L.A. phenomenon has put at least a small crimp in that flaunting of wealth: motorized muggers who follow Rolls drivers home to rob them in their driveways.

And, it would seem, Los Angeles cannot offer enough urban problems, either natural or manmade, to prevent more people and more automobiles from going there. That is not truly puzzling, since nature has blessed the place with almost year-round warmth and its people have made it an exciting and economically thriving city. Moreover, the ubiquitous automobile puts almost all of L.A.'s residents within a couple of hours' reach of the snow-clad mountains in one direction and the sandy Pacific beaches in another.

As befits the ultimate city of a nation of immigrants, most of the newcomers of Los Angeles lately have been of foreign origin. Since 1970, more than two million immigrants have settled here, leading one demographer to compare the city to the old immigrant-processing facility in New York Bay: "There is no question that it is the new Ellis Island."

The new arrivals have come mainly from Pacific-rim nations such as Mexico, El Salvador, the Philippines, Taiwan, Vietnam and Korea. As recently as 1960, only one in nine Los Angeles County residents was Hispanic, and just one in 100 was of Asian descent. By the mid-1980s, almost a third of the county's 7.9 million population was Hispanic and a tenth was Asian. Whites made up less than half the population, which meant that *everybody* living in Los Angeles County was a member of a minority group. It would be difficult to conceive of a more American situation than that. □

LOVE AFFAIR WITH THE OPEN ROAD

To drive across the United States on one of its many superhighways is to know how the nation lives—forever in motion. Founded by people on the move, America has grown up as the most mobile country on earth, its inhabitants traveling by train, by plane, but most of all in roaring streams of motor vehicles such as those at right. In America, where some four million miles of paved highways carry an awesome total of 170 million cars, trucks and buses, the open road means far more than simply transportation.

Every day of their lives, most Americans spend at least some time on the road. What other nation would build 40,000 motels, sell billions of hamburgers from roadside fast-food chains, or pick up its alcoholic beverages at drive-through liquor stores?

The road that may best reveal the U.S. character is Interstate 80, a double ribbon stretching 3,000 miles from coast to coast with not one stop light. Starting with the grumble of Manhattan's commuters, I-80 plunges through the heart of Middle America—gritty mill towns and tiny islands of horse-drawn America—to climax in a sweep of plains and mountains leading to San Francisco Bay.

A stacked highway sign on Interstate 80, a main artery of the 42,500-mile, 56-billion-dollar U.S. superhighway system, offers a compelling invitation to a restless nation in love with its automobiles.

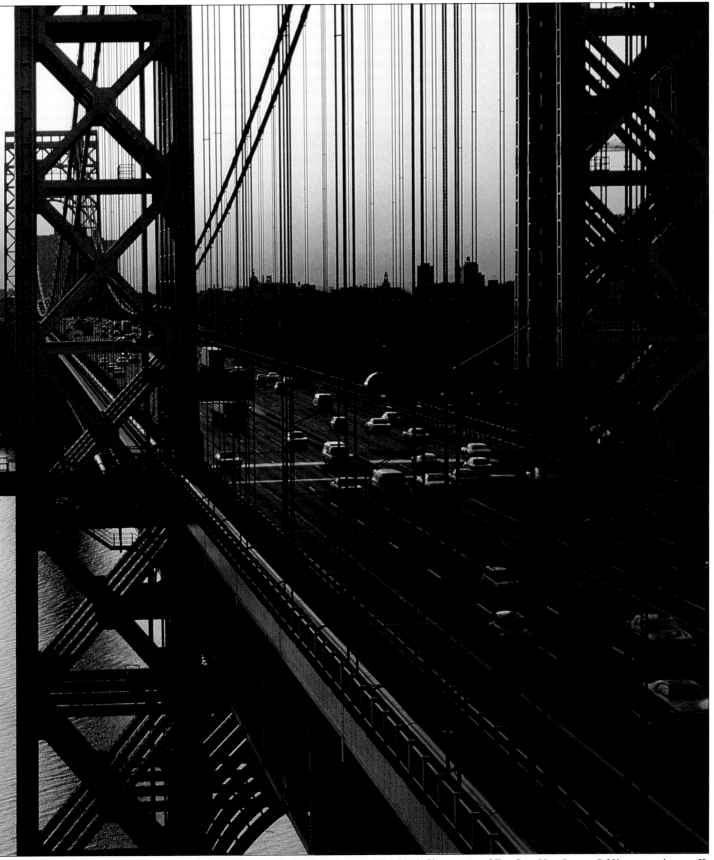

The George Washington Bridge carries dawn traffic over the Hudson between New York City *(rear)* **and Fort Lee, New Jersey, I-80's eastern jump-off.**

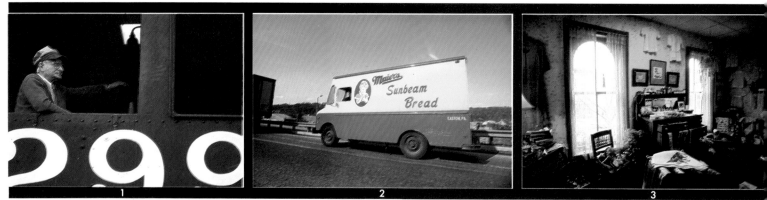

1. Wearing the railroadman's traditional cap, an engineer peers from the cab window of a diesel locomotive rolling alongside Interstate 80 at Paterson, New Jersey, 20 miles west of the George Washington Bridge.
2. A brightly colored van carries bread into the Pennsylvania countryside from a central bakery in Easton, Pennsylvania. Across the U.S., trucks such as this and its big-brother trailer rigs haul about a billion ton-miles of freight every year.
3. A cozy antique shop in Stroudsburg, Pennsylvania, displays its potpourri of quilts, pillows, spices, dolls and children's clothes. A quiet resort town, Stroudsburg nestles three miles from the spectacular Delaware Water Gap, which cleaves the wooded Kittatinny Mountains.
4. Tendrils of smoke trail away from the stacks and towers of a steel plant along Ohio's Mahoning River. In one stretch along its banks, mills and Bessemer converters stand cheek-by-jowl for a distance of 20 miles.
5. Two steelworkers stroll out the gate of a Youngstown, Ohio, mill at day's end. Skilled hands such as these still produce a third of the world's steel, and 15 per cent of all their output goes into America's motor vehicles.
6. A Chicago bartender in a bar like thousands of others along I-80 smiles behind the barrier that distances him from his customers, enabling him to perform the bartender's time-honored role of listener.

4   5   6

The Great Falls at Paterson, New Jersey, boom between the frames of a venerable bridge and some modern graffiti. The United States' first planned industrial town, Paterson was laid out in 1791 by statesman Alexander Hamilton.

1 An Amish mother in Indiana,
clad in the old-fashioned bonnet and
other plain clothing required by
her religious sect, a branch of the
Mennonites, adjusts the mantle
of a gas lantern. The Amish shun
most modern trappings, but may
compromise on appliances such as
stoves and refrigerators.
2 A covered bridge on a snowy byway
near the superhighway, in Madison County, Iowa, is preserved as a
reminder of the days when people traveled by horse and buggy and
sheltered under its long roof
when caught out in a storm.
3 Iowa livestock-raiser George
Mueller chortles happily as he embraces a stuffed bison (also
called buffalo) head and the decorat-
ed skull of a longhorn cow.
Though he specializes in cattle,
Mueller also grazes bison, whose
wild ancestors once roamed the
West by the tens of millions.
4 A mailbox whose post has been cut
and painted to represent Uncle
Sam stands in the snow outside a
frame house in Iowa, in the farm
country that stretches into the rich
prairie on either side of I-80.
5 Two University of Nebraska students play pinball and video games
in the Student Union recreation
room in Lincoln, capital of Nebraska. From Lincoln to the Pacific,
I-80 parallels the route of America's
first transcontinental railway.
6 Scout's Rest, in Nebraska, served as
the winter quarters of Buffalo
Bill Cody, the one-time Indian-
fighter whose Wild West Show
toured the world in the late 19th and
early 20th centuries. He once
slaughtered 4,000 buffalo in the area
over a 17-month period.
7 A massive grain elevator towers
above the one- and two-story buildings of Gothenburg, Nebraska —
named after the Swedish city by the
Scandinavian pioneers who led
the migration of Northern and Central Europeans to the region.

Amish buggies, still the prescribed means of everyday travel for their owners, stand near a barn in LaGrange, Indiana. In the mid-19th century thousands of Amish came to the Midwest from Pennsylvania farms.

1 In a parking lot just off I-80 in Wyoming, heavy trucks await their drivers outside a McDonald's fast-food stop, whose golden-arch insignia appears above the cab of the most distant rig.

2 A proud trucker taking a break shows off a T-shirt caricaturing his trade. Two-way citizens-band radios and even husband-wife driving teams have alleviated the boredom of long-haul driving.

3 The symbol of a cowboy riding a bucking horse on the license plate of a Wyoming vehicle announces that this is cattle country. Second in the West only to Montana for livestock breeding, Wyoming has 1,400,000 head of cattle and fewer than 500,000 people.

4 The Eagle Gate, a landmark on State Street in Salt Lake City, Utah, frames the state capitol. Rising in the distance are the Wasatch Mountains, whose winter snow cover provides virtually all the water for this thriving desert city of 160,000.

5 The brilliantly lighted Mormon Temple, focal point for the Church of Jesus Christ of Latter-day Saints, rises above the trees of Temple Square in the heart of Salt Lake City. Devout, energetic and prosperous, Mormons traditionally send their young adults on two-year missions across the United States and overseas.

6 Bespectacled Minnie Dick, a Western Shoshoni woman, works at handcrafts in her home on the South Fork Indian Reserve along Nevada's Humboldt River. Rising in snow-capped mountains, the Humboldt grows shallow and disappears in the sand and clay of Nevada's desert interior.

4   5   6

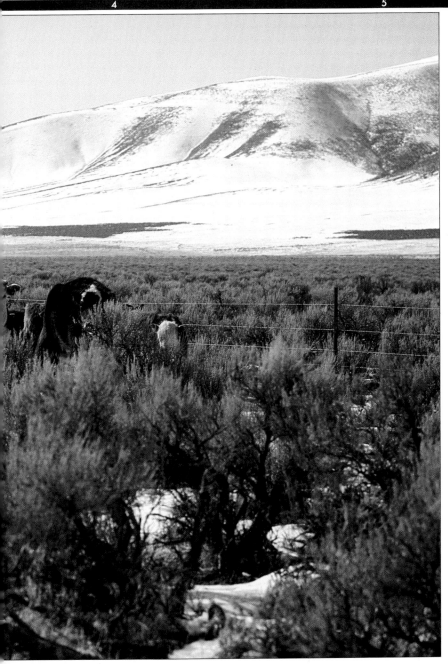

A handful of mixed range cattle
stare toward the highway from a
field of sagebrush and snow. On the
high plains of the West it takes
10 acres of such sparse land to
sustain a single steer.

1 Not far from I-80, a gas station in
   the backwater of Golconda, Nevada,
   crouches forlornly in the late
   afternoon sun, its sign empty and its
   water tower a skeleton of girders.

2 A hurry-up wedding chapel in
   Reno, Nevada, adorned with
   neon hearts, awaits its bustling
   trade. Though more famed for
   gambling and for jiffy divorces that
   require only six weeks' state residence, Reno annually sees eight
   times as many weddings take
   place as marriages sundered.

3 Ghost-town resident Louise
   Buckingham plays with two cats
   clinging to a picket fence in the
   mud and melting snow of Paradise
   Valley, Nevada. She lives in the
   remains of the town hotel with her
   husband, Fred — whose father, a
   prospector, founded the town
   around the turn of the century.

4 This snowbound cemetery holds
   former inhabitants of another
   Nevada ghost town, Tuscarora,
   north of I-80. The high plains
   and mountains of the West are spot-
   ted with abandoned mines and
   towns, the residuum of gold and silver strikes of the 19th and early
   20th centuries.

5 A Tahoe resident blasts his
   snowmobile through the winter forest. Snowmobilers here — as elsewhere — are under constant pressure from environmentalists, who
   object to exhaust pollution and the
   disruption of wildlife in the ecologi-
   cally fragile mountain region.

6 A waitress serves up drinks at a
   Lake Tahoe restaurant, on the border between California and Nevada.
   Many such young women double as
   ski instructors during the area's
   five-month winter-sport season in
   the surrounding mountains.

7 An icicle-draped motel stands
   isolated in the snowy heights of the
   Sierra. The clientele includes gam-
   blers and senior citizens who stay
   here to take in Lake Tahoe's casinos
   and night life.

4

5

6

7

The westbound lane of I-80 stretches
string-straight to the horizon of
Nevada's snow-speckled desert land.
Since 1960 the U.S. has spent
$300 billion on building and
maintaining its highways — more than
on anything else except defense.

1   2   3

1 A bright haze hangs above the
water on the California shore of
Lake Tahoe. More than two
thirds of the 22-mile-long, 12-mile-
wide lake lies within the borders
of California; the remainder is in
the state of Nevada.

2 Skiers tired from a day on the slopes
of the High Sierra wallow in the
hot water and steam of a whirlpool
bath. There are about 10 major
ski resorts that lie within 20 miles of
Donner Pass, where I-80 cuts between 10,000-foot peaks.

3 A green landscape near the Napa
Valley, a leading wine-producing
region, contrasts dramatically
with the ski country only a few miles
to the east. Such geographic vari-
ance is characteristic of California,
where subarctic mountain peaks,
hot desert areas and temperate en-
claves adjoin.

4 Oil tanks line the highway as I-80
nears California's coastal range.
Some of America's largest petroleum deposits lie in California and
its offshore fields, giving the state
an annual oil production of 385
million barrels.

5 A modified A-frame country
home, with a private airplane
parked outside, nestles amid the
rounded hills of the coastal mountains. Real estate has long been
a prime investment in California,
where an influx of newcomers
helps to boost sales.

6 Three bearded, beaded young
men pass a bemused onlooker in
San Francisco's Haight-Ashbury
district. The city's population is a
microcosm of cosmopolitan California — wealthy businesspeople,
Asian families, Italian fisher-
men, Hispanic émigrés, university
people and a restless legacy of
street hippies from the 1960s.

On the last mile of its journey from the East Coast, I-80 soars grandly upon the Oakland Bay Bridge, alight in the early evening, with the city of San Francisco for a backdrop.

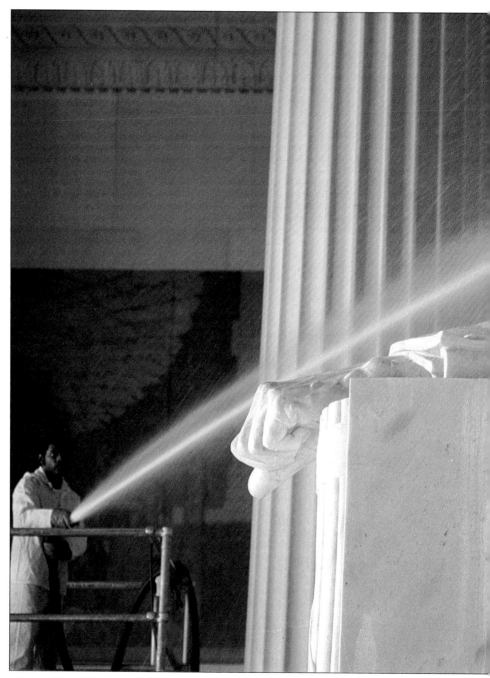

Abraham Lincoln's craggy visage
receives an unceremonious bath to
remove accumulated grime. More
than three million visitors a year come
to see the marble statue in
Washington, D.C.'s Lincoln Memorial.

SEEKING A MORE PERFECT UNION

The tension is still there in the faded words on parchments preserved in the glass cases of the National Archives. First, the Declaration of Independence. It is unequivocal and direct. "All men" have "unalienable Rights," it says, to "Life, Liberty and the pursuit of Happiness." Government exists to secure those benefits — and when it fails to do so, the people have the right "to abolish it, and to institute new Government." There is no mistaking the background noise: the sound of guns making a revolution.

In another display case is a document that begins, "We the People of the United States, in Order to form a more perfect Union, establish Justice, insure domestic Tranquility . . . and secure the blessings of Liberty . . . do ordain and establish this Constitution. . . ." This one is talking about creating a government, not abolishing one, about nailing down liberty by restricting it in some ways. Absolute liberty must be hedged in order to guarantee union, justice and "Tranquility," a word that is intriguingly different from the Declaration's "Happiness."

Liberty and order, the individual's pursuit of happiness, and society's quest for tranquillity: These are the sometimes conflicting aims that Americans have been attempting to reconcile through more than two centuries of growth and change. The history of the nation has been, and continues to be, a nonstop balancing act between abstract ideals and pragmatic needs.

The debate over the rival claims of liberty and order goes back to the very seedtime of the nation. By 1634, ten thousand of the English religious dissidents known as Puritans had established a colony in Massachusetts. Their leader was a successful lawyer, John Winthrop, who had forsaken his comfortable estate in order to worship God in the wilderness as he saw fit. He endorsed the Puritan notion that a proper society was one governed by magistrates, chosen exclusively by male church members. To them alone God would reveal his ideas of proper administration. All others would be "free" to obey the government of God's servants.

Even for some Massachusetts Puritans, that was too strong a medicine. Roger Williams, though a clergyman, was wary of uniting the powers of church and state. What would happen, he asked, when reasonable people disagreed on God's meaning? If one side used the authority of government to beat down its opponents, that would be just like the tyranny from which they had all tried to escape. Williams wanted to let people alone in matters of conscience, and to give all of them a share in rule. Governments, he contended, should have "no more power than the people shall betrust them with."

Massachusetts leaders voted Williams out of the colony in 1635. A few years later they did the same to the first of a long procession of strong-

2

minded Yankee women, Anne Hutchinson, whom Winthrop uncharitably labeled "the American Jezebel." Her sin was to argue that God might hint his intentions directly to an individual believer (of either sex) rather than only to the magistrates. Williams and Hutchinson and their exiled followers founded a new colony, Rhode Island, where the separation of church and state was eventually guaranteed by law.

Williams' experiment in democracy was the exception, at least for a time. Other early colonies along North America's Atlantic coast were set down by companies or proprietors chartered by the English Crown. They were intended to make a profit for investors, and they were not meant to be run democratically. They were instead to be administered by authorities in London. But geographical and historical logic pushed the English colonies toward liberty and self-government. For one thing, high-handed rule by proprietors or royal officials would discourage settlers, who had to be enticed to face the hardships of the wilderness by the promise of having a measure of freedom to run their own affairs (the glaring exceptions were African slaves, who were being brought into the Southern colonies as early as 1619).

For another, many of the English newcomers had lived through a period of struggle between king and Parliament that was capped in 1689 by the enactment of British laws that included such guarantees as trial by jury, no taxation without Parliament's consent, and immunity from arbitrary seizure of property. When the heirs to this Parliamentary revolution went overseas, they expected to take with them these hard-won "rights of freeborn Englishmen," or they would not go at all.

On paper, the English colonies still appeared to be run from London by administrators with autocratic powers. But in fact by 1760 they were close to being self-governing republics, with colonial assemblies in which different factions fought legislative battles over who should benefit from land, tax, currency and trade policies.

The British government proceeded unwittingly to make a nation out of these disparate political communities by an ill-considered attempt to tighten up imperial administration. King George III issued proclamations, and Parliament passed various acts between 1763 and 1775 designed to raise revenue through new taxes, to enforce rules against smuggling and to prevent settlers from moving westward, encroaching on Indian territory and provoking Indian wars. The British government, unaware of how strongly the colonists would resent the imposition of such edicts, was scarcely prepared for the resulting tidal wave of outraged reaction.

From Boston to Charleston, colonists denounced such interference as positively un-English, submitting petitions ringing with determination that freeborn Britons should not be made slaves. They staged boycotts, demonstrations and riots — and when the British cracked down with tough new enforcement policies in 1775, resistance turned into revolution. A representative body, the Continental Congress, with members drawn from all 13 colonies, met in Philadelphia and took on the job of running a war.

Even while the guns were blazing away, many colonists continued to hope that their gracious sovereign would grant them autonomy within the empire. But as it became evident that King

George was quite willing to allow his red-coated troops to shoot down his overseas subjects, colonial resolve to be independent stiffened. Minds were changed, too, by Thomas Paine's best-selling 1776 pamphlet, "Common Sense." Paine, who had come over from England only two years earlier, described George III as "the royal brute of Great Britain." He argued that "in free countries the law ought to be king; and there ought to be no other." The onetime colonists should transform themselves into "the FREE AND INDEPENDENT STATES OF AMERICA."

The Continental Congress embraced that idea and shortly expressed it in the more formal terms of the Declaration of Independence. Five more years of hard battlefield struggle was needed to win the war and make the claim of independence good. But finally, in 1782, Britain agreed to a peace treaty. The 13 former British outposts had become the United States of America. Loosely united under a concord called the Articles of Confederation, the Americans grappled with the question of how to govern themselves.

Were they now a single people requiring a single government, or was America an association of independent states? A strong central government was probably necessary to win respect and security in the world, but might it not swallow up the liberties it was supposed to protect? What liberties ought to be protected, anyway, and whose?

These were the fundamental issues faced by the 55 men who gathered in Philadelphia in the spring of 1787 to revise and "improve" the Articles of Confederation, and ended up instead writing the Constitution. They were a remarkably well-educated group, predominantly young, but heavily experienced in pragmatic politics. Almost all of them, including the "Federalists," who argued the case for strengthening central government, had learned to be suspicious of power, from King George's heavy-handed use of it. And even those who spoke for light controls on the popular will recognized that individuals were mainly moved by self-interest and could not always be trusted to bear in mind the common good.

What they contrived was a set of compromises that divided power between the states and a strong central government, which would be checked by a theoretically equal division of authority between executive, legislative and judicial branches (page 118). Even so, Antifederalists believed the document gave government too much control.

To meet such objections, the first U.S. Congress in its first regular session in 1789 fashioned 10 constitutional amendments, the Bill of Rights, spelling out the limits on governmental power. These clauses confronted the government with a series of "thou shalt nots." Thou shalt not interfere with the free exercise of religion, or of speech. Thou shalt not deny trial by jury, nor engage in unreasonable searches of the people's dwellings or possessions. Finally, thou shalt not claim any authority not specifically spelled out in the Constitution; all powers not mentioned there are "reserved to the states . . . or to the people."

The Constitution, at least until the Bill of Rights was added, was not quite democratic enough for free-thinking Thomas Jefferson, but he accepted it as the best that could be achieved at the time. It was too democratic for conservative New York lawyer Alexander Hamilton, but he, too, would settle for it as an attainable half loaf. These two men were brilliant exponents of totally opposed views of America's meaning. That both could work within the Constitution's deliberately open-ended framework is the best possible illustration of how superbly flexible and well-wrought the document was.

Jefferson was the first of a breed of patrician democrats, privileged Americans who embraced popular ideals. He was an uncommon defender of commoners—a planter, musician, survey-or, architect, attorney and inventor, who held that government was best when it governed least. He was suspicious of the tendency of all governments to usurp and abuse power and believed that a rebellion every now and then would be a healthy thing ("the tree of liberty," as he put it, needed periodically to be refreshed "by the blood of patriots and tyrants").

Hamilton was self-made. The illegitimate son of a West Indian merchant,

A CHRONOLOGY OF KEY EVENTS

15,000-10,000 B.C. The first inhabitants of the New World arrive in Alaska via the Bering Strait, and spread down and across the Americas.

1500 B.C.-1500 A.D. Specialized cultures arise among the peoples Christopher Columbus would misname "Indians."

c. 1000 Viking Chief Leif Erikson explores the North American east coast.

1565 Spanish explorers found St. Augustine, Florida, the first permanent European settlement.

1607 Jamestown, Virginia, the first permanent English colony, is founded.

1619 Virginia elects the first legislative assembly. The first blacks — 20 indentured servants — arrive.

1620 Pilgrims arrive aboard the *Mayflower;* they establish a colony at Plymouth, Massachusetts.

1636 Harvard, the first college in the colonies, is founded.

1664 The British seize New Amsterdam and rename it New York. Maryland's "black code" declares all blacks in the colony to be slaves for life.

1675-1678 King Philip's War: New England Indian tribes attack settlements, trying to halt expansion by Europeans.

1682 French explorer Robert Cavalier de la Salle claims the Mississippi River valley with all its tributaries for France, naming the vast territory Louisiana for King Louis XIV.

1704 The first regular newspaper, *Boston News Letter,* appears.

JOIN, or DIE.

1754 At the Albany Congress, Benjamin Franklin uses the slogan "Join or Die" *(above)* to draw support for his Plan of Union, designed to protect the colonists' mutual interests. Although the plan is not ratified, it presages the federal union.

1755-1763 French and Indian War. At the war's end France gives up its possessions in the Ohio and Mississippi River valleys.

1764 Parliament's Revenue Act to tax the colonists results in their boycott of the imported items.

1767 More taxes are levied by Parliament, including one on tea. Colonial protests and boycotts spread.

1770 The Boston Massacre: five people are killed by British troops.

1773 The cargo of an East India Company ship is thrown overboard at the Boston Tea Party *(above).*

1774 English ships blockade Boston Harbor; Parliament annuls the Massachusetts government charter. The First Continental Congress issues a Declaration of Rights, calling for civil disobedience.

1775 Minutemen engage advancing British troops at Lexington and Concord *(below).* The Second Continental Congress appoints George Washington Commander-in-Chief.

1681 Quaker William Penn founds Pennsylvania, which offers religious liberty under its progressive Charter of Privileges *(above).*

1765 The Stamp Act goes into effect and violent opposition to it breaks out. Radical groups called Sons of Liberty are formed.

1776 The Declaration of Independence is approved on July 4.

1777-1780 Colonial forces win key battles. In 1777 the Stars and Stripes replaces a temporary flag that had incorporated the Union Jack.

1781 British General Charles Cornwallis, besieged at Yorktown by Washington's forces and their French allies, surrenders his entire army.

1787 The Northwest Ordinance establishes procedures by which territories can become states.

1789 The Constitution is ratified and Washington is elected president. The first Congress meets. The Supreme Court is established.

1791 The first 10 amendments of the Constitution, known as the Bill of Rights, are put into effect.

1803 The western boundary of the U.S. is advanced to the Rocky Mountains with the purchase of the Louisiana Territory, by President Thomas Jefferson (above).

1812-1814 War with Britain over free trade and sailors' rights.

1817-1825 The Erie Canal, built with immigrant labor, connects the Great Lakes and New York Harbor.

1820 The Missouri Compromise permits slavery in Missouri but bars it in the rest of the Louisiana Purchase, north of 36° 30' N.

1823 The Monroe Doctrine bans European interference in the Americas.

1845 Texas is annexed by Congress; the Mexican War results.

1848 Mexico cedes Texas, California, Arizona, Utah and Nevada to the United States as war ends. The California gold rush begins.

1855 Armed clashes occur in Kansas over the slavery issue.

1857 The Supreme Court's Dred Scott decision denies blacks constitutional rights on the grounds they are not and cannot be citizens.

1859 Radical abolitionists seize the federal arsenal at Harpers Ferry under the leadership of John Brown. Brown is captured and hanged for treason.

1860 Abraham Lincoln (above) is elected president. South Carolina secedes from the Union over the issue of states' rights.

1861 The Confederate States of America are organized. Fort Sumter is bombarded. The Civil War begins, pitting brother against brother (below).

1862 Lincoln issues the Emancipation Proclamation. The Morrill Act provides land grants for state colleges.

1863 Victories of the North in the Gettysburg battle and the Vicksburg campaign are turning points of the war.

1865 The Civil War ends as Confederate General Robert E. Lee surrenders to Union General Ulysses S. Grant at Appomattox. Lincoln is assassinated by actor John Wilkes Booth.

1867 Alaska is purchased from Russia.

1868 The 14th Amendment is ratified, giving civil rights to blacks.

1869 The first transcontinental railroad, built with immigrant Irish and Chinese labor, is completed.

1876 Alexander Graham Bell invents the telephone.

1879 Thomas A. Edison invents the incandescent light bulb.

1886 Twenty years' warfare with Western Indians comes to an end with Apache chief Geronimo's surrender. The American Federation of Labor is formed and becomes the spearhead of the American labor movement.

1896 The Supreme Court upholds Southern segregation laws, "separate but equal" treatment of blacks.

1898 The Spanish-American War. Spain cedes the Philippines, Puerto Rico and Guam to the U.S., and guarantees Cuba's independence. Congress annexes the Hawaiian Islands.

1901 President William McKinley is assassinated; 43-year-old Theodore Roosevelt becomes the youngest United States president.

1903 The Wright brothers make the first successful powered flight, at Kitty Hawk, North Carolina.

1916 The Virgin Islands are purchased from Denmark.

BUY A LIBERTY BOND

3RD Liberty Loan

1917-1918 U.S. forces fight in World War I *(above).*

1920 The 18th Amendment goes into effect, prohibiting the sale of intoxicating liquors. Female suffrage is guaranteed by the 19th Amendment.

1924 Congress confers citizenship on American Indians.

1927 Charles A. Lindbergh makes the first nonstop solo flight across the Atlantic *(above).*

1929 The U.S. stock market collapses,

touching off a prolonged and worldwide economic depression.

1933 President Franklin D. Roosevelt *(above)* launches the "New Deal," which speeds the nation's economic recovery through social and economic reforms. Prohibition is repealed.

1941 The U.S. enters World War II after Japan bombs Pearl Harbor.

1942 Japanese-Americans are interned under the War Relocation Act.

1945 Germany surrenders. President Roosevelt dies; Harry S. Truman succeeds him. Atomic bombs are dropped on Hiroshima and Nagasaki; Japan surrenders.

1948 Congress passes the European Recovery Plan (the Marshall Plan).

1950-53 The Korean War.

1954 The Supreme Court unanimously bars racial segregation in the public schools, in its *Brown* v. *Board of Education* decision.

1955 Martin Luther King Jr. leads a successful boycott of the segregated bus system in Montgomery, Alabama.

1959 Alaska and Hawaii become states.

1962 John Glenn becomes the first American to orbit the earth.

1963 President John F. Kennedy is assassinated in Dallas, Texas; Lyndon B. Johnson succeeds him.

1964 The Civil Rights Act goes into effect. U.S. planes begin combat missions over South Vietnam.

1967 Thurgood Marshall becomes the first black Supreme Court Justice.

1968 Martin Luther King Jr. is assassinated in Memphis, Tennessee. Robert Kennedy is shot in Los Angeles. The number of U.S. soldiers in Vietnam *(below)* climbs to half a million.

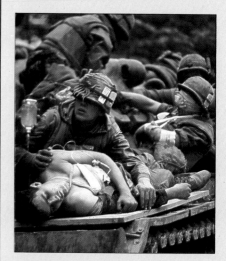

1969 The first U.S. astronauts land on the moon.

1972 The Watergate scandal begins.

1973 The Vietnam War ends with the signing of a four-power peace pact.

1974 President Richard Nixon resigns over Watergate; he is pardoned by President Gerald Ford.

1976 The nation's bicentennial. President Jimmy Carter is elected.

1980 Ronald W. Reagan becomes the nation's 40th president.

1981 U.S. hostages are freed after more than a year in captivity in Iran. The space shuttle makes its maiden voyage. Sandra Day O'Connor becomes the first woman appointed to the Supreme Court.

1986 The space shuttle Challenger explodes, killing all seven on board.

he had come to North America only in 1772, but by 1776, at the age of 26, was already chief aide-de-camp to George Washington, commander of the revolutionary forces. Hamilton's political philosophy was tough and conservative. "All communities divide themselves into the few and the many," he said. The "few" were the "rich and well born." The rest were "the mass of the people." What government needed, above all, was stability, and the way to get it was to give the rich "a distinct, permanent share in the Government."

Hamilton and Jefferson both served in the Cabinet of George Washington, who was the nation's choice as the first president. As secretary of the treasury, Hamilton carried out his policy of making the national government the friend of the rich. He set up a national bank to control lending and prevent the inflation that would have devalued the holdings of the well-to-do. He encouraged manufacturing through subsidies and protective tariffs. And he showed that the government meant business by using federal troops in 1794 to crush a small Pennsylvania rebellion against an excise tax on liquor. (Outraged Pennsylvania farmers just wanted to distill their grain and sell it as good, tax-free Monongahela whiskey.)

Jefferson, meanwhile, quit his post as secretary of state to help organize a coalition that would fight Hamilton's policies. He failed in his attempt to become president as the candidate of the newly formed Democratic-Republican party in 1796. The job went instead to John Adams, Hamilton's ally from Massachusetts. Adams, Hamilton and their Federalist party proceeded to justify Jefferson's growing anxieties about the new government's despotic tendencies. Especially alarming was the passage,

during what proved a short-lived crisis, of the Alien and Sedition Acts of 1798, which gave the president and the courts broad powers to expel foreigners and jail political critics.

Yet at that very point, when the young Constitution seemed in peril, it proved equal to the crisis. In 1800 the Democratic-Republicans won the election, and the Federalists dutifully turned over the reins to Jefferson, who responded in his inaugural address with a wound-healing call for national unity. The "peaceful revolution" of 1800 was a landmark. It proved that bitterly opposed political factions could battle on, election by election, within the framework of the Constitution and without bloodshed.

Further tests were in the offing, caused largely by the wild surge of expansion that swiftly followed the conclusion of a second conflict with Britain, the War of 1812. Between then and 1860, by purchase, annexation and war, the United States added more than two million square miles of territory to its original 890,000. In that same half century the population swelled, largely through immigration, from seven million to just over 30 million. By 1860 the original 13 states had increased in number to 33. At any time during the period there would have been truth in the remark made in 1817 by the South Carolina politician John C. Calhoun: "We are rapidly — I was about to say fearfully — growing."

Early in this explosive era, what seemed a new sort of rugged, highly individualistic American began to emerge, especially on the Western frontier, where settlers were unfettered by the traditions of the older Atlantic seaboard society or even by very much government. The uninhibited

Westerners demanded a greater voice for their growing region in the policies of the government in Washington. One way to get it was to enlarge the franchise, with every man having the vote. During the early decades of the century a number of states — all of which had originally restricted voting rights to male property owners — passed universal manhood suffrage acts, although the emphasis was still on "man," and meant only "white man." The broadened electorate promptly provided the nation with a president who became the symbol of the age, Andrew Jackson.

He was markedly different from the scholar-politicians of the founding generation. Born dirt-poor in the Carolinas in 1767, he had taught himself law and moved to frontier Tennessee in the 1780s. There he became a prosperous community leader. When his neighbors elected him a judge, he expressed his judicial philosophy in these simple terms: "Do what is right between parties. That is what the law means." He embodied what a later historian would call the characteristic American qualities bred by the frontier experience: "coarseness and strength combined with acuteness and inquisitiveness; restless, nervous energy; dominant individualism, working for good and for evil, and that buoyancy and exuberance which comes with freedom."

Jackson had become a national legend as a commander of frontier troops in the War of 1812: In the last battle of the war, his sharpshooters virtually annihilated advancing British columns at New Orleans. In 1818, he again demonstrated his gift for military boldness by leading an invasion of Florida — Spanish territory at the time — without authorization from Washington.

There, Jackson rooted out a pair of

British traders who were inciting the Seminole Indians to raid settlements in Georgia; he set up a court-martial and executed the two.

Frontier folk loved it and, to the horror of Eastern conservatives, helped elect their hero president in 1828. Jackson proved a decisive chief executive, active on behalf of the people and especially those of his own Western region. His hostility to monopoly and privilege caused him to battle and destroy the Bank of the United States, which had controlled the money supply. With the bank's demise, the credit that the farmers needed became easier to get. He opened land for settlement — unfortunately at the expense of the Indians. Above all, Jackson embodied the idea that ordinary Americans, not just Eastern aristocrats, were capable of running the country.

Although Jackson advanced the cause of true equality in America, there was much left to do. Inevitably, the country's most glaring violation of human rights, black slavery, became the focus of national attention. Antislavery movements had existed since colonial times, but they had generally proposed moderate solutions such as gradual emancipation, with slaveholders being compensated for their loss of property.

A new, immoderate tone was brought to the slavery debate by William Lloyd Garrison and his newspaper, *The Liberator.* An editor and printer from Massachusetts, Garrison was fiercely self-righteous and in no way conciliatory. "I am in earnest," he wrote in *The Liberator's* first issue in 1831. "I will not equivocate — I will not excuse — I will not retreat a single inch; and I will be heard!" Slavery, he said, must be ended immediately, completely and without compensation. His war cry — and it would prove nothing less — was soon echoed by dozens of fellow abolitionists.

The abolitionists were right, of course; the continuing forcible enslavement of four million black human beings was an intolerable wrong, especially in a nation supposedly dedicated to freedom and equality. But most Southerners did not see it that way. The South's entire economy, founded on cotton grown for export, was dependent on a reliable source of cheap labor. Further, many Southerners regarded slavery as a "positive good." Their slaves were better off, they said, than white mill hands shackled by economic necessity to the looms and lathes of Northern factories. Besides, the slaves were benefited spiritually and morally by the Christian faith they learned from their masters.

As this debate raged in pulpit and press, the growth of the nation inexorably brought the issue to a head. New states, most of which banned slavery, were formed and admitted to the Union as the people expanded westward. By 1850 nonslave states outnumbered those that had slavery, and all the free states together had a total population 50 percent greater than that of the slave states. The South's new minority status meant that the rest of the country possessed the legislative power, should it wish to use it, to outlaw slavery everywhere, or to attack any other uniquely Southern institution.

This was a prospect particularly frightening to Southerners such as the brilliant but resolutely conservative John C. Calhoun. In his last speech as a senator, in 1850, he uttered a dire warning: Unless the North agreed to changes to restore the "equilibrium" between the sections, it would be evident that its objects were "power and aggrandizement." The South would then have no choices but "submission or resistance."

Calhoun wanted nothing less than federal guarantees that slavery would never be outlawed, not only in the states, but also in the still sparsely settled Western territories, where the American future lay. That, in its turn, was intolerable to Northern moderates like Abraham Lincoln, a poor-born, self-taught lawyer who struggled to reconcile his frank hatred of slavery with his profound respect for the Constitution, which clearly protected slavery in those states that wanted it. Slavery, said Lincoln, denied the basic promise of the Declaration of Independence, the "promise that in due time the weights would be lifted from the shoulders of all men and that all should have an equal chance."

In the proposals of the new Republican party, founded in 1854, Lincoln found a middle ground that he hoped would avoid war. Slavery could continue in the states that already had it,

where it would probably die gradually as the progressive spirit of the age caught up with the South. But it must not be allowed in the Western territories, which should be consecrated to "free labor." This compromise, however, was wholly unacceptable to Calhoun's successors in the South's leadership. The positions of the two sections had become irreconcilable.

Lincoln's election to the presidency in 1860 was taken as a signal in the South that it was futile for the region to remain in the Union. Eleven Southern states quickly seceded and formed the Confederate States of America. The North took up arms rather than see the Union destroyed. Lincoln's often-quoted words, delivered in Gettysburg, Pennsylvania, in 1863 made clear that the Civil War, to Northerners at least, was not a mere sectional struggle but a momentous test of whether a nation "conceived in Liberty, and dedicated to the proposition that all men are created equal" could "long endure."

Paradox abounded. Slavery was at

Striking a warlike pose, a Confederate volunteer, Private William B. Todd of the 9th Virginia Cavalry, holds his pistol at the ready in an old ambrotype. The Civil War saw ghastly slaughter; one out of every four men who served perished.

the root of the war, but the North did not begin combat with any avowed intention of ending slavery. Southerners insisted that their basic cause was not preservation of slavery but simply self-determination — the cause of the colonies in 1776. In the end, the necessities of war destroyed what the South called its "peculiar institution." Lincoln freed the slaves by proclamation in 1863, partly because Northern public opinion demanded it, partly to help recruit blacks into the Union armies and partly to convince the people of Britain and other European countries, which had been inclined to aid the South, that the North was fighting a "moral cause."

By the end of the bloody conflict, in 1865, the North was in a mood of mingled idealism and vengefulness. The states ratified not only the 13th Amendment to the Constitution, abolishing slavery everywhere, but also the 14th and 15th, conferring citizenship and suffrage on all male Americans regardless of race — with the single, glaring exception of Indians, who had to wait until 1924.

The latter two amendments proved hard to enforce. After 11 years of occupation of the beaten South, federal troops were withdrawn as the North turned back to business as usual. Blacks, left to the untender mercies of the white Southern majority, were quickly relegated to a distinctly inferior status, for the most part without votes, without equal rights and without the law's protection of their property or even their lives.

Still, the war had been a victory for the ideal (if not the fact) of equality and established that the nation could and would "long endure." Both sides had resorted to battle in the name of freedom. But one of the freedoms the

2

Confederates wanted was the freedom to deny freedom to others. Nothing more tragically illustrated the difficulty of reconciling different American notions of individual liberty and social good than the 500,000 lives lost in the sectional struggle.

The war's end liberated new whirlwinds of energy. Pioneer farmers poured into the West. Using new machines, they produced grain and livestock that booming Western cities such as Minneapolis, Kansas City, St. Louis and Chicago transformed into enough flour and canned meat to feed millions. Roaring blast furnaces in Pennsylvania poured out rivers of molten iron and steel. Everywhere Americans heard the clang and hum of machines that mass-produced typewriters, streetcars, shoes and carpets, furniture, clothing and other goods.

In this increasingly industrialized society, which numbered 75 million people by 1900, the Constitution framed for an agrarian republic of four million was strained once again. The men who controlled the new mechanical marvels boasted that their success was evidence of what exceptional individuals could do, given enough freedom. These preeminent beneficiaries of the *laissez-faire* economy included men like Cornelius Vanderbilt, who went from illiterate ferryboatman to railroad mogul in a lifetime of hard bargaining and of ruining his competitors; and John D. Rockefeller, a pious but ruthless bookkeeper who skillfully amassed oil wells, eventually forming the huge Standard Oil Company, the colossus of the petroleum industry.

Such men frequently did not do corporate contest with their competition. Instead they formed alliances, or simply bought out their competitors, creating combinations called "trusts" that totally controlled whole industries. These individuals wielded prodigious power — power to rig prices, pay workers the lowest possible wages or even throw entire communities out of work. They bought newspapers to propagate their opinions and shamelessly bribed judges and legislators. The gulf between them and those who worked for them — coal miners crushed or gassed in unsafe mines, children dragging themselves through the drab alleys of company towns to work 12-hour days — grew wider and wider.

Liberty had led to a gross inequality, aptly described in the 1892 platform of the People's party, a short-lived political organization of wheat and cotton farmers radicalized by hard times and falling prices. "From the same prolific womb of governmental injustice," the Populists said, "we breed the two great classes of tramps and millionaires."

The pendulum of democratic thinking inevitably swung back toward asserting society's right to intervene on behalf of the powerless. Some citizens pressed their case by independent organization, without waiting for government to stir itself to redress injustices. Workers who joined the growing labor movement during the late 19th century, in fact, often had to fight government as well as employers, because laws that protected the freedom of entrepreneurs to make money denied working people their freedom to organize unions and to strike.

The chief political impetus for reform came from what was called the Progressive movement. The Progressives were men and women who were born or raised after the Civil War and who carried the humanitarian and evangelistic impulses of the abolitionists and other early crusaders into the industrial age. Through their zeal, state

AN AMERICAN TRAGEDY

The opening of the West, a great American saga, had its dark side. It drove the Indians from their land, even in areas set aside by treaty as refuges. The Treaty of Laramie typified the process of dispossession. Signed *(far right)* by Red Cloud and his fellow chiefs in 1868, it gave the Sioux and other tribes about half of present-day South Dakota. But the pact, like so many others, was not kept. Gold lured white miners into the refuge's Black Hills, which the Sioux held sacred. Outraged Indians attacked, and war ensued. Eventually the entire preserve was usurped. In 1871 Congress scrapped all the treaties and began setting up the much-reduced Indian reservations that exist today.

Chief Red Cloud sits for a photograph in 1880.

and city statute books were soon peppered with new laws (bitterly opposed by the big corporations) requiring health and safety inspections of factories, compensation for job-related injuries or deaths, and limits on the hours that women and children could work. Slowly the country edged toward control of industrial evils.

But the movement needed a major champion if it was to achieve its ends at the federal level. Progressivism found its national leader in Theodore Roosevelt. A man of enormous energy and self-confidence, Roosevelt came from New York's old mercantile aristocracy. Overcoming weak eyes and childhood asthma, he turned himself into a rugged physical specimen who was forever hiking, hunting, riding, boxing and playing tennis. Before he became vice president at the age of 42, in 1901, Roosevelt had already been New York City police commissioner, assistant secretary of the navy, commander of a cavalry regiment in the Spanish-American War and New York governor.

When the assassination of President William McKinley put Roosevelt in the White House, he turned his talent for zestful action to a crusade against concentrated corporate wealth. The only weapon available to him was a blunt instrument, the Sherman Anti-Trust Act of 1890. It declared "combinations in restraint of trade" to be illegal, but it had been rarely enforced — except against labor unions. Roosevelt ordered the Department of Justice to employ the Act against monopolies by initiating antitrust suits. The department promptly did so, dismembering a railroad combine engineered by J. P. Morgan, E. H. Harriman and James J. Hill, three of the nation's most powerful millionaires.

Roosevelt then turned to giving organized labor a boost. He settled a major coal strike by forcing the mine owners to sit down with a union representative in Washington, D.C., thus officially recognizing labor's right to negotiate. He crusaded for other reforms. From what he called the "bully pulpit" of the White House, he lent his weight to journalistic exposés of tainted meat and poisonous patent medicines, and secured passage of the Pure Food and Drug Act. He fought diligently for conservation, closing millions of wilderness acres to commercial exploitation.

But beneath the turbulence of his reforms, Roosevelt steered a basically moderate course. He might denounce "the representatives of predatory wealth" as guilty of "all forms of iniquity from the oppression of wage workers to defrauding the public," but he was selective about what trusts he tried to bust. He saw some corporate combinations as inevitable and a tolerable format for non-monopolistic industries.

Chiefs meet government delegates, mostly army officers, at Fort Laramie, Wyoming, to sign a short-lived territorial treaty.

65

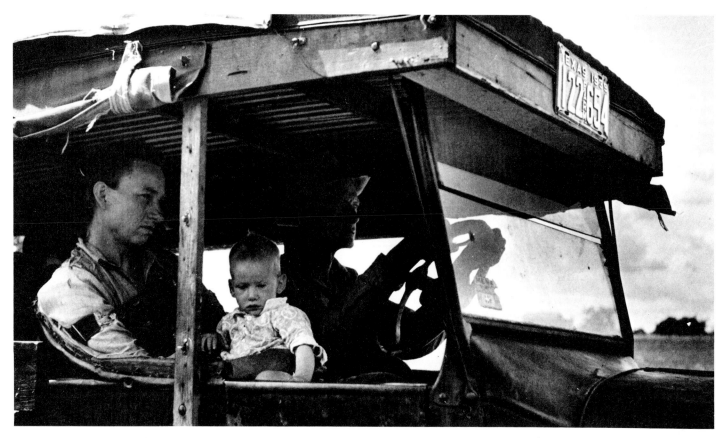

His aim was to save the soul of the nation only from the extremes of wealth and poverty, promising Americans what he called a "Square Deal."

Roosevelt left the White House in 1909 after two terms as president, but when conservatives gained control of the Republican Party in 1912 he ran again under the banner of a new, third party: the Progressives. The party platform called for a number of reformist measures, including federal regulation of corporations, the prohibition of child labor, unemployment insurance for workers and national standards for industrial health and safety.

Roosevelt lost the election to Woodrow Wilson, the Democratic candidate. But some of the principles of the Progressive party were adopted by Wilson, himself a reform-minded exemplar of progressive attitudes. Just as the Antifederalists had managed to get 10

amendments into the U.S. Constitution and the abolitionists three, the Progressives succeeded in adding three between 1913 and 1920. The 16th created the income tax, which could (and later did) become an instrument for the reallocation of wealth through heavier taxes on higher incomes. The 17th provided for the direct election of senators (formerly, they were chosen by their state legislatures). The 19th gave votes to women, thanks largely to female leadership in the Progressive party. (The 18th, repealed after 13 years, prohibited the manufacture or sale of alcoholic beverages.)

World War I and the economic prosperity that followed in the Roaring Twenties temporarily sidetracked the impulse toward reform. But in the early 1930s a worldwide depression savaged the American economy. By 1932 one quarter of the work force was on

the streets and half the country's productive machinery was idle. Capitalism seemed to be on its last legs and America was swept by alarmist talk of revolutions. The country needed a fresh dose of ideas for reviving the general welfare. It got them from Franklin Delano Roosevelt.

This Roosevelt, known by the press as F.D.R., was only a distant cousin of the former president, but he shared much of the same Rooseveltian energy and political skill. On taking office in 1933 he captured the faith of most Americans with bold words and bold deeds. "The only thing we have to fear," he told them, "is fear itself," and he at once began pushing through Congress a radical collection of programs that he termed a "New Deal."

Some of his programs were primarily emergency measures designed to patch up a badly wounded economy. The job-

Their eyes revealing more defeat than hope, a weary family sets off from Oklahoma in 1939 in quest of a better life. During the Depression, thousands of families left the Dust Bowl, a region of prairie farmland ruined by overuse and erosion.

less were put to work on a multitude of government-financed public projects. They built courthouses, post offices, bridges, dams, airports and thousands of miles of roads. By reforestation and flood control, they reclaimed millions of acres of soil from erosion and devastation. The New Deal was literally stamped on the American landscape.

Other programs reflected long-term reform principles. Taken as a whole, the New Deal amounted to a peaceful revolution that, for all the enmity it elicited from conservative businessmen, preserved and strengthened the private-enterprise system while bringing the federal government into direct, significant and almost daily contact with the citizenry. A New Deal agency, the Securities and Exchange Commission, still guards investors against fraud in stock and bond markets. The National Labor Relations Board (set up in 1935) still protects the right of workers to collective bargaining. Every Social Security payment to the elderly and disabled is the result of an act passed under Roosevelt's leadership in 1935.

Both the Square Deal and the New Deal were variations on the theme of promoting the well-being of the people as a whole. Other presidents played the tune again under various titles, from the end of World War II into the 1960s. Harry Truman had his Fair Deal, John Kennedy his New Frontier, and Lyndon Johnson his Great Society. But the 1960s were marked by another sort of ferment that recalled those strenuous searches for individual liberty, coupled somehow with equality, that had characterized earlier periods of American history.

It was leftover business from the Civil War, in fact, that was largely responsible for the new period of unrest. In 1954, the Supreme Court ruled that the segregation of black children in their own separate public schools was unconstitutional. That long-deferred decision provoked strong resistance among whites in Southern communities, but it inspired a new generation of black men and women to a new attack on the barriers that surrounded them.

They found nonviolent but effective ways of dramatizing their demands — the sit-in, the boycott, the mass march, the demonstration — under the leadership of a young black clergyman, Martin Luther King Jr., whose eloquence touched the national conscience. His work secured the passage of strong federal civil-rights and voting-rights acts in 1964 and 1965, and won him a Nobel Peace Prize in 1964. It also, in 1968, brought an assassin's bullet.

Roger Williams, seeking separation of church and state in Massachusetts in the 1630s, and Martin Luther King Jr., struggling for equal rights for all in the 1960s, were linked by a chain of American tradition: the belief that government exists mainly for the purpose of protecting individual rights. The black revolt proved contagious. Women, Native Americans, Hispanics, homosexuals and other groups previously denied admission to the mainstream of American life organized themselves to demand a fair share of power. Equality, they said, was for everybody.

The success of these movements renewed in many Americans a confidence in their ability to influence their nation's course. They challenged the very authority of their elected government at every unpopular turn. With the help of a Congress newly responsive to the people's will, they brought an end to a disliked war in Vietnam, persuaded one president (Lyndon Johnson) not to run for reelection and compelled another (Richard Nixon) to resign before completing his term of office.

As the protest movements mounted in volume, they provoked an inevitable backlash. Some critics questioned the wisdom of placing congressional constraints on the president's authority to use military force or secret operations in pursuit of the country's aims abroad. Others challenged domestic programs created to afford opportunities to long-frustrated minorities. Should the government, they asked, offer special help to one group of citizens, even from the worthiest motives, at the expense of others?

Moreover, each new civil-rights guarantee required new enforcement machinery, so that the weight of government seemed to some to be growing oppressively heavy. This produced its own backlash against all the years of reform and the bureaucracy that went with it. Followers of the Progressive gospel began to find the going hard.

But when reform was challenged, it was almost always challenged in democratic terms. Many of the debates of the 1980s — on the limits of governmental powers, on a woman's right to have an abortion, on prayer in schools — came down in the end to the same enduring root questions. What can government do to help all Americans achieve the blessings of liberty? And what must it refrain from doing to make sure that each person enjoys as fully as possible both liberty and the right to pursue happiness?

The language that rings out from the television sets and in print is contemporary, but the issues at the heart of the discussions would not be unfamiliar to John Winthrop, Thomas Jefferson, John Calhoun or Abraham Lincoln. □

Henry G. Wilks	Ricanthony R. Ashley	Dino D. Dutcher	Lisa K. Wallace
Polish	Jamaican	Italian	American Indian
German	Spanish	English	English
Scottish	American Indian	Irish	German
American Indian	French		Irish
Irish	English		
English	African		

CHILDREN OF THE MELTING POT

Americans are proud of their varied ancestries. Just how diverse these can be is suggested by the lineage of the members of a typical squad of cadets *(above)* at the United States Military Academy at West Point, New York. The family trees of these nine young men and women show a total of 14 ethnic strains, ranging from English, German and Irish to African and American Indian.

Certain strains are stronger than others in the population as a whole. According to the latest census, some 50 million Americans, about one fourth of the United States population, are of English

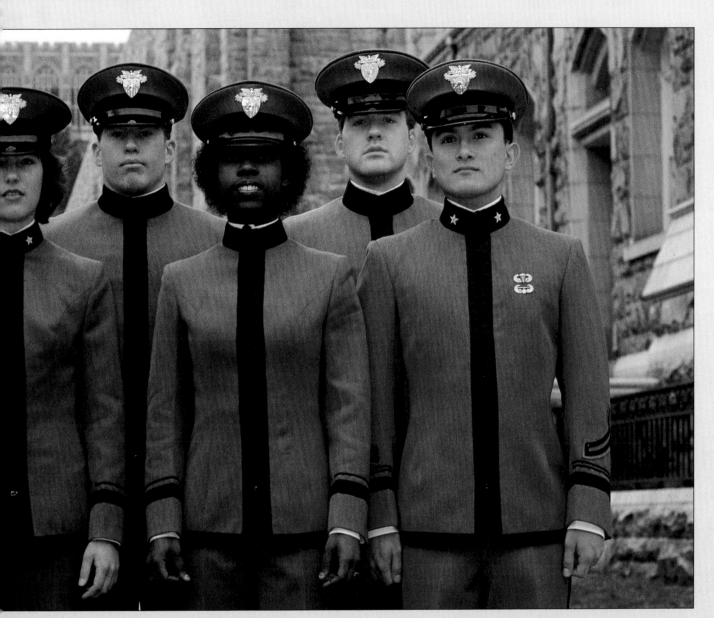

Leslie A. Lewis
French
Welsh
German
Irish

Kevin A. Moore
Icelandic
Scottish
Irish

Jamie L. McCloud
African
American Indian

William F. Willoughby
German
English
Scottish
Irish

John T. Snider
Japanese
German
Irish

descent — more people than live in England today. Another 49 million citizens identify themselves as of German ancestry, a number equal to almost two thirds of the population of East and West Germany. Americans of Irish descent, 40 million strong, outnumber by 12 to 1 the population of the Republic of Ireland.

The peak period of immigration for Europeans was the six decades from 1871 to 1930, when 30,385,000 men, women and children arrived on America's shores; in one 10-year stretch, 1901 to 1910, almost nine million were admitted. In the later decades of this century, immigration has slowed but by no means halted. From 1941 through 1979, there were 10.8 million new arrivals, who enriched the nation's ethnic mix further. More than 215,000 Vietnamese now consider the U.S. their home, as do 120,000 Iranians and 90,000 Haitians.

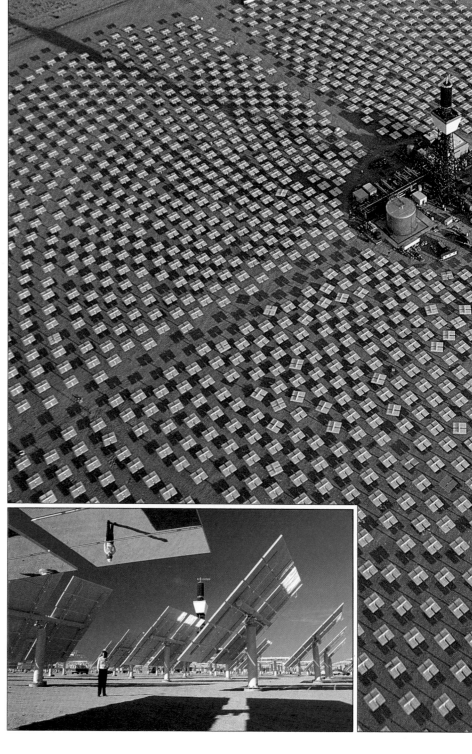

At the first and largest solar electrical generating plant in the U.S., located in the California desert, more than 1,800 sun-tracking mirrors, or heliostats, surround the 300-foot-high power tower. Each heliostat *(inset)* beams reflected sunlight at the boiler atop the tower to produce steam, which drives a turbine.

AN ECONOMY OF ABUNDANCE

In 1807, a Connecticut clockmaker by the name of Eli Terry contracted to make the parts and assemble the movements for 4,000 grandfather clocks at the unheard-of low price of four dollars apiece. The buyer would construct the clock cases and market the finished product. Many of Terry's fellow clockmakers thought he was out of his mind. Making a clock was an intricate process involving such traditional hand tools as hammer, saw, file and drill. Even with the help of an apprentice or two, a master craftsman could produce only about 20 clocks a year, each of them selling for about $50.

Terry had been in the business for 15 years; he knew that traditional methods would not allow him to turn out 400 clocks, let alone 4,000, in the three years allotted him. But he had a bold plan. He intended to use machines to shape each component of the clockworks to a standard pattern and size. Then these interchangeable parts could be quickly assembled into complete movements. The idea was not new: A fellow Connecticut entrepreneur, Eli Whitney, was attempting to use a similar system to produce 10,000 muskets for the U.S. government. But Terry was the first to apply the notion to a consumer product.

With the help of two apprentices, Terry converted an old gristmill. By a system of shafts and belts, he harnessed the mill's water wheel to the lathes, saws and other tools that would turn out the interchangeable clock parts. He went into production, and by the final year of the contract, he and his apprentices could manufacture more clock movements in a day than a comparable work force could make by hand in a year. His total of 3,000 movements for that year fulfilled the contract. For perhaps the first time in history, true mass production of a household mechanical device had been achieved.

Even with mass production, however, the elaborate grandfather clock was still beyond the pocketbooks of most Americans. So Terry designed a new clock that was only 20 inches high — small enough to stand on a shelf. By mass production and effective marketing, he was able to sell this model directly to customers for only $15, a price that made it possible for the average American to own a clock.

The techniques of mass production pioneered in the U.S. by Eli Terry and others formed the foundation for what later became known as the "American system" of manufacturing. The concept of mechanized, large-scale production quickly spread beyond the walls of the factory, transforming work in such other sectors of the American economy as mining and, above all, agriculture. Terry, one historian has written, was "the last of the craftsmen and the first of the industrialists."

The United States in the early 19th century was ripe for such innovation. The land was brimming with natural

71

3

resources from which things could be made in great quantity; Terry, for example, made his clock movements from wood instead of brass because timber was abundant and cheap. Moreover, there was a market for goods in quantity. The nation was open to trade, and its commerce was unhindered by the tariff barriers that divided and hobbled the European economy.

And the American people hankered after a better life. Terry knew instinctively that not just the wealthy but any farm family might be induced to buy a clock if it was inexpensive enough. As American historian David Potter has observed, "European radical thought is prone to demand that the man of property be stripped of his carriage and his fine clothes. But American radical thought is likely to insist, instead, that the ordinary man is entitled to mass-produced copies, indistinguishable from the originals."

Producing goods in quantity was only the beginning. The same forces led inevitably to what became another dominant feature of the U.S. economy, the provision of services en masse. At first, services — work that in itself does not produce a commodity — centered upon transporting the goods and selling them. Later, as industry became highly efficient, the proportion of the work force needed to produce goods declined: An increasing number of people went into education, health care, government, communications, and restaurant and hotel management, helping to fulfill ever-rising American expectations of the good life.

By the 1980s, in fact, the provision of services had long since displaced the production of goods as the principal economic activity in the U.S., employing nearly 70 percent of the 100-million-member working labor force. In 1985 the total output of goods and services — the country's gross national product, or GNP — amounted to a staggering $4 trillion, or roughly one fourth of all the goods and services produced in the world.

The result is a standard of living rivaled by few other nations. In 1985, the U.S. per capita income was $11,727, one of the highest among industrialized countries. By the mid-1980s, 77 percent of all American households had a washing machine, 43 percent a dishwasher, 45 percent a freezer, and 98 percent had telephone service.

Some of America's prosperity, of course, is attributable to two world wars that dislocated other countries' economies while actually spurring growth in the U.S. But wartime booms cannot account for all or even most of the extraordinary gains in productivity over the years. From 1909 to 1985, the output per paid worker-hour in U.S. factories increased four and a half times. Such gains must be credited not only to the invention of better machines, but also to advances in the training of workers and managers. Down through the years America has spawned or lured from abroad thousands of resourceful industrial pioneers who — driven by ambition for wealth or power, or by the plain thrill of doing something better than anyone had ever done it before — have put the nation at the forefront of technological progress.

The roster of American business geniuses includes men like Andrew Carnegie, a Scottish immigrant who became a steelmaker in 1872. The steel industry at that time was a shambles of small companies — each specializing in one stage of production, from ore smelting to making finished goods —

FINANCIAL HEART OF THE FARM BELT

The United States is a nation of investors: An estimated one out of every five Americans owns stock. For the intrepid, there are riskier forms of investment, such as trading in commodities — grain, meat, precious metals and dozens of other products. In a typical commodities transaction, investors buy and sell "futures" — contracts to deliver or take delivery of large amounts of goods at a later date and at the price fixed in the contracts.

The risk is great because commodity prices can fluctuate wildly; an unexpected cancellation in a large export sale can send wheat prices plummeting, hurting investors who bought contracts at higher prices. Futures can also soar or drop from minute to minute in response to rumors and investors' hopes and fears concerning supply and demand. Clever speculators can make a million dollars in a single week of buying and selling futures. And millionaires have lost fortunes just as swiftly.

The nation's most active commodities exchange is the Chicago Board of Trade (right), which also deals in financial instruments such as Treasury bonds. It was founded in 1848 by 82 Chicago merchants to provide a central trading facility for the Midwest's grain farmers. Establishing prices for crops not yet harvested (or even planted) led to the trade in futures. Today the Board of Trade is housed in a huge building in downtown Chicago. It has more than 3,000 members, some of them independent speculators and some traders who act for brokerage houses and wear colored jackets to indicate the firms they represent.

Life in the stepped-down octagonal "pits" where the individual commodities are traded is grimly serious. "It's ferocious," one trader has said; "it's man against man." Said another: "There are no friends in the pit. You do not take prisoners in here."

As a tally board records prices *(top left)*, traders jam one of the floors of Chicago's Board of Trade.

A janitor cleans up the debris after a furious trading session in one of the Board's pits *(above)*. At right, soybean traders with membership badges use hand signals to execute orders. Here the man with four fingers extended and palm outward is selling four soybean contracts, or 20,000 bushels.

3

and middlemen who bought and resold the partially processed metal at every stage. Worse, the manufacturers did not know their running costs; they discovered whether they had made a profit or lost money only at the end of the year, when their books were balanced.

Carnegie cut out the middlemen by combining all steps of production in his company. By careful measurement of materials, fuel use, man-hours and equipment life, he determined his true costs—applying, in short, what modern business calls cost accounting. And he drove those costs down by reinvesting his profits in new machines whenever he found any that could make a product faster or with less manpower. He once tore down a rolling mill

only three months old when he learned of a new design that would make production cheaper.

Over a span of 28 years Carnegie cut the cost of making steel by almost four fifths. By 1900 his company was producing almost as much as the entire British steel industry, and his profits were 20 times as great as they had been only 12 years earlier.

American industrialists of the 20th century added their own innovations to the accomplishments of men like Terry and Carnegie. This was especially true of leaders in the automobile industry, which in time became the country's biggest. In 1901 one of the early carmakers, Ransom Eli Olds, fused the system of using interchangeable parts

with an idea from the meat-packing business, where beef traveled on overhead trolleys as it was processed. The result was the very symbol of modern mass production: the automobile assembly line. Cars under construction moved past workers, each of whom added a part or parts. In 1904 Olds produced 4,000 of his Oldsmobiles, a phenomenal number for the era.

Four years later Henry Ford improved on Olds's system by breaking down the assembly process into eversmaller and ever-simpler tasks, each of which was handled by one person and with as few motions as possible. Off the end of the line rolled the Ford Model T, the car that put America on wheels and touched off the explosive growth of the U.S. automobile industry. The first Model T took 12 hours and 28 minutes to assemble; by 1914, Ford had the time down to 93 minutes. Thanks to improved production methods, the retail price of a Model T dropped 49 percent over a five-year period, putting the car within the financial reach of the average American family. Henry Ford's devotion to cost-cutting led him to avoid all frills; he used to say the customer could have a Model T in any color he or she wanted, "so long as it is black."

Ford's technical achievements enabled him to dominate the auto industry until the 1920s, when a genius of a different stripe, Alfred P. Sloan Jr., applied his own brilliant insights to a company called General Motors, or GM.

General Motors was then run by William C. Durant, a wheeler-dealer who made crucial decisions by intuition as he juggled the receivers of the 10 continually ringing telephones that crowded his desk. Sloan, a vice president of the company, despaired over Durant's haphazard management, which was bringing GM close to ruin.

Sloan proposed a restructuring of GM that would disperse authority and ensure that decisions were made only after careful consideration of the facts. Durant took no notice, and Sloan was about to resign, when the Du Pont Company, a giant munitions manufacturer and one of the firm's major stockholders, became alarmed about GM's shaky condition. It forced Durant out and later installed Sloan as chief executive officer.

Sloan immediately began delegating authority to the heads of GM's various divisions while building a strong central staff to set policy and make market forecasts. He preached a new concept of profitability: The amount of money a company earns is less important than the ratio of that profit to the invested capital. This notion of "return on investment" became gospel to American business. Sloan also devised perhaps the most successful commercial sales gimmick in history; he started the practice of visibly altering automobile models every year, unashamedly admitting he wanted "to make you dissatisfied with your current car so you will buy a new one."

Good managers like Sloan knew the value of creative talent, and American industry — as well as the U.S. government — has for most of the 20th century hired idea people and devoted huge sums of money to research and development. Out of such research has come a dazzling list of products, including plastics, nylon and polyester — synthetics that revolutionized the packaging and clothing industries and today find thousands of applications around the world.

Occasionally a new product will come along that consumers never knew they needed until its sudden appearance in the marketplace. A case in point is the instant camera. It was invented by Edwin Land, a Harvard University dropout who in a brief career obtained more than 500 patents, an achievement second only to that of the most prolific of American inventors, Thomas Edison.

Since 1888, when George Eastman introduced his inexpensive Kodak box camera and made everyone a photographer ("You press the button, we do the rest"), few Americans had felt any great need for film that could be developed on the spot. Then one day in 1943, Edwin Land's three-year-old daughter, Jennifer, asked why she could not see immediately the photograph that he had just snapped of her.

Why not, indeed? Land had already demonstrated his inventive genius, devising a sheet of polarized plastic that could be used in sunglasses and camera filters to cut down on glare. Within an hour of Jennifer's question, Land had worked out in his head the design of a camera that would in effect compress in its innards the apparatus of an entire darkroom. His instant camera, which was five years in the making, is now the basis of a two-billion-dollar-a-year industry that serves such markets as medicine and electronics as well as amateur photography.

There are few more dramatic examples of the benefits of research than the stunning breakthroughs in electronics. American predominance in this field dates back to 1947 and the development of the transistor by scientists at the Bell Telephone Laboratories, the world's largest industrial research organization. The transistor could control and amplify electric signals much faster and more efficiently than the old bulky vacuum tubes that had been widely used since the early 1920s. Over the next three decades, such devices were made ever-smaller and speedier. By the 1980s, thousands of microscopic transistors were being routinely inscribed on individual flecks of silicon no bigger than the thumb of a newborn baby. Known as integrated circuits — or chips — these slivers of silicon can store tens of thousands of bits of information. Other chips, called microprocessors, contain both the memory and the logic functions of a complete computer. At a cost of $25, one microprocessor can do the work of a computer that as recently as 1960 sold for $100,000.

Reductions in production costs made

Industrial robots send out crackling sparks as they weld automobiles in a Delaware assembly plant. The robots cost $100,000 each, but 30 of them can weld as many as 100 cars an hour, a 60 percent improvement on the output of the same number of human workers.

3

the new computer-based "high technology" economical not only for large businesses but for many thousands of small firms and — through relatively low-priced personal computers — millions of households as well. Thus, at a time when the old "smokestack" industries, such as steel and automobile production, were declining because of foreign competition and other forces, a new mass market for high-tech goods and services was created. The new market spurred enormous industrial growth in places such as Boston and the area south of San Francisco known as Silicon Valley. For example, California's Intel Corporation, which developed the first microprocessor in 1971, mushroomed from just 42 employees in 1968 to 21,000 in 1985.

That is just the way most Americans believe their economy is meant to function — as a marketplace where competition for the consumer's dollars encourages innovation, and entrepreneurs with good new ideas can become millionaires almost overnight. Such a picture of the U.S. economic system, however, is not complete. Although the United States probably comes closer than any other Western country except West Germany to having a pure free-enterprise economy, it is still true that government — at the federal, state and local levels — plays a large role in that economy. Government is the biggest spender, dispensing 28 percent of the gross national product and absorbing, in the form of taxes, 20 percent of that product to pay for its operations.

The government's effects on the economy are myriad and all-pervasive. Since the 1950s, the federal government has tried to reduce fluctuations in the business cycle by the use of fiscal policy (taxation and government

The ultimate human-computer interface is demonstrated in Berkeley, California, during a whimsical sales promotion for word processors. Eight million home computers were in use in the U.S. by the mid-1980s.

spending) and monetary policy (controlling the money supply via the quasi-independent Federal Reserve System, which functions much like the central banks of European countries).

During business recessions, the government has pumped demand into the flagging economy by spending more or taxing less — or both — thus expanding its budget deficit. During periods of economic growth, it has attempted to curb its deficit. But in the quarter century following 1957, the federal government succeeded in balancing its annual budget only twice. Its tendency to create ever-larger deficits has often been blamed for driving up interest rates and pushing private borrowers — companies seeking money for expansion, or individuals who want loans for new houses or new cars — out of the credit markets.

In recent years, monetary policy has played an increasingly prominent role in government attempts to stabilize the

economy. While the government has achieved some success in leveling out the boom-and-bust cycles of earlier eras, its economic policies have not eliminated the pattern of accelerating inflation alternating with painful recession. Many people suspect the government's efforts often have compounded the problems.

Fiscal and monetary policies are not the only areas in which government is involved in the American economy. Government regulates business to ensure competition, and to protect the interests of workers and consumers. Almost all Americans have some pet gripe about government interference with their economic freedom. But just about all also have reason to be thankful for the government's involvement in the economy (although they rarely say so out loud) or to ask for even more involvement. Magazine and book publishers cherish their favorable mailing rates. Steelworkers and automobile manufacturers ask for tighter import controls to protect them from foreign competition. Truckers and oil companies resist higher taxes while pleading for more of the tax-supported highways that help make them prosperous.

The sector of the American economy in which government has been most directly involved — with results both good and bad — is agriculture. American farmers are the most productive the world has ever known. In 1850, one U.S. farm worker produced enough food and fiber for four persons; by the 1980s one worker produced enough for 78. Though they constitute only about 3 percent of the U.S. labor force, 3.4 million farm workers feed and help clothe the entire nation and much of the rest of the world. U.S. farmers produce 64 percent of the world's soybeans, 46 percent of its corn, 21 percent of its meat and 17 percent of its wheat. So much is left over after taking care of America's own substantial appetites that nearly one third of the annual farm production is shipped abroad.

This astonishing success stems in part from American agriculture's unrivaled natural blessings: a favorable climate and vast stretches of fertile soil. But it also has to do with government's long-standing involvement with agriculture. The government gave away land to settlers. It established agricultural colleges and a network of county agents to develop more efficient ways of nurturing crops and animals and to teach these new ways to farmers. It promoted the electrification of farms and subsidized extensive irrigation projects (about one fourth the total value of U.S. farm production comes from irrigated land). And for decades it has provided low-interest loans to farmers.

Government research, in combination with private research, has led to quantum leaps in the science of farming: new, higher-yielding hybrid plants and animals; supercharged fertilizers; chemicals that rid fields of weeds and insects; artificial-insemination techniques and embryo transplants that improve livestock.

Today U.S. agriculture is a high-tech industry where productivity has grown much more rapidly than in any other sector of the economy. In contrast to the romantic image of man and the earth, the American farmer is likely to spend less time with his hands in the soil than the average suburban gardener. He may plan his crops with the aid of a home computer, plant his fields on a huge, 300-horsepower tractor, and irrigate them with a turbine-powered sprinkler that can water about 133 acres at once. Today, tractors on U.S. farms outnumber workers.

Ironically, government intervention to aid agriculture has created a serious problem: Federal price-support pro-

Haitian workers plant celery seedlings in the deep, black soil of the Glades, 882 square miles of rich bottom land created when part of Florida's swampy Everglades was drained. As an almost-year-round supplier of a variety of vegetables, the area has come to be known as the "winter salad bowl."

77

3

grams have led to tremendous surpluses. Had agriculture been left to free-market forces, constantly increasing farm production would have resulted in such low prices that many American farmers would have gone broke. Those who survived could then have demanded higher prices for their crops. That would have hurt the food-buying American consumer — until the higher prices again inspired farmers to produce yet more, driving prices down again and condemning more farmers to financial ruin.

Since 1933, the federal government has tried to stabilize prices at a fair level for farmers by a variety of programs. These have included stepping in to buy up surpluses when prices dropped too low, paying farmers subsidies to take land out of production, selling surpluses abroad or giving them away to hungry Third World countries, and issuing food stamps, with which America's poor could purchase food they could not otherwise afford.

The results have been mixed. The United States can give away only a limited amount of food abroad or at home without harming the agricultural economy of another nation and its own as well. Yet the notion of paying farmers to refrain from producing food when a large proportion of the world's population, including some Americans, go to bed hungry each night seems immoral to many people.

Some farmers complain that the government has not gone far enough to support agricultural prices and help them stay in business. But at least the federal programs seem to have slowed the rate of reduction in the number of farmers as productivity increased.

The government's programs certainly did not stop that reduction. In 1950,

Weed-covered levees trace sinuous patterns through a paddy field in California's Sacramento Valley. Most of the 340,000 acres of California that are devoted to rice cultivation are sown by airplane.

3

15.3 percent of Americans lived on farms; by the mid-1980s, the figure had shrunk to just 2.4 percent. During that period the average farm more than doubled in size, to about 450 acres, and this enabled it to make efficient use of new technology. The number of farms, meanwhile, declined by more than half, from 5.6 million to 2.3 million.

Even this statistic fails to convey the full extent of the changes down on the farm. The true working farms are now vastly outnumbered by weekend hobby farms for the well-to-do, or part-time operations that supplement wages earned from jobs in town. Only about 20 percent of all farms have annual sales of $40,000 or more, yet they are responsible for nearly 80 percent of U.S. agricultural production.

Farms fall into two basic categories by ownership: family farms and corporate farms. Despite repeated predictions of the demise of family-owned farms, they still account for nearly 90 percent of America's agricultural acreage and 82 percent of sales. While some farmers continue to diversify, producing grain, a variety of livestock and vegetables *(pages 84-91),* most find greater profits in specialization. They produce only pigs or cattle or chickens or grain, and often they concentrate on one stage of the production of their chosen specialty, such as fattening hogs.

Farms like these form the base of the multibillion-dollar-a-year structure of enterprises collectively known as agribusiness. The interest a farmer pays on

At Chicago's huge O'Hare Airport, a sleek jet airliner taxies along a ramp built over a high-speed traffic artery. O'Hare handles so much air traffic that, on average, a plane lands or takes off every 52 seconds.

loans supports the local bank; the tractors he buys help sustain the dealer and the manufacturer; the fattened hogs he takes to market provide business for the meat-packer as well as the supermarket. Agribusiness employs more than 23 million people, or 22 percent of America's labor force, and has fostered a new breed of entrepreneur.

Abraham Neufeld, who owns a farm in central Kansas, goes one step further than the specialist—he does not even farm his land. He rents out his 200 acres to a neighbor and earns his own living from a fleet of six combine harvesters. Each of these machines—26 feet long and 13 feet wide—can cut and thresh 3,000 bushels of wheat a day. Every May, Neufeld and his family gather up a small group of hired hands and begin a four-month pilgrimage. They move from Oklahoma north to the Canadian border, contracting their harvesting service to farmers who find it more profitable to hire someone like Neufeld than to own and operate such expensive machinery themselves.

Each harvester has a soundproofed, air-conditioned cab with a stereo to entertain the driver and a computer to monitor the machine's operation and warn him if anything goes wrong. The Neufelds harvest about 20,000 acres of wheat every summer, then switch attachments on the machines and set off to cut many acres more of late-maturing corn.

Where the nature of the agricultural product lends itself to the economies of truly large-scale production, corporate farms have become increasingly dominant. In the production of cane sugar and cotton, for example, the necessary investments in land and technology are out of reach for most family farmers.

Corporations also have made inroads into the raising of other crops. In California's San Joaquin Valley, Tejon Agricultural Partners (TAP) utilizes the latest in technology on 13,000 acres planted with wine grapes, pistachios, walnuts and almonds. The company mechanically harvests its entire nut crop and 50 percent of the wine crop. To maintain ideal fertilizing and irrigation conditions, it routinely analyzes plant tissue for nutrients and measures soil moisture with a special electronic device. TAP also maximizes its use of equipment. Because of the farm's size, fewer machines per acre are needed to work the land.

A creation of high finance that would dumbfound even a sophisticated family farmer, TAP is the offspring of a larger corporation, which owns real estate, oil reserves and other businesses. Through the help of this parent company, TAP was able to commit large amounts of capital to the farm. And unlike many individual farmers, it could afford to wait the eight to ten years needed to see a reasonable profit on that investment. TAP had a further advantage; it could employ experts in cost accounting, entomology and field-crew management to monitor expenses, fight pests and increase efficiency. Most family farmers must either take on such tasks themselves or hire consultants to do these jobs.

American farming, in spite of all its amazing productivity, actually constitutes a very small slice of the nation's economy. Agriculture, forestry and fisheries put together account for only about 3 percent of the country's gross national product.

The biggest sector of the economy—and the fastest growing—is that of service industries. In the mid-1980s, the service industries accounted for 67 percent of the U.S. gross national product. In one service-industry category, eating and drinking places, the increase in the number of jobs from 1970 to 1981 amounted to more than the total 1981 employment in the automobile and steelmaking industries combined.

Since service industries do not turn out any tangible products—goods—some people wonder whether a service-oriented economy can actually increase its total wealth, or even survive for long. Author Mark Twain pointed out about a hundred years ago that no society could prosper soley by its people "taking in each other's washing." John Nevin, chairman of The Firestone Tire & Rubber Company, recently restated Mark Twain's viewpoint in modern terms: "The idea that we can have an economy by selling hamburgers to each other is absurd."

Services, in fact, are a whole lot bigger than that. They include businesses like insurance and banking, which accumulate funds that can be invested in manufacturing companies. Other service industries—mail-order houses, department stores, supermarket chains—are essential to the distribution and selling of the goods produced by manufacturers. Services such as health care (a $287-billion-a-year business in 1981) and education ($181-billion-a-year in 1981) assist American productivity in all industries by keeping managers and workers well, and by preparing their children for life in an increasingly complex economy.

The service industries that play the most important role in the American economy are those that come under the general heading of marketing. This category embraces all the business activities involved in directing the flow of goods and services to consumers and

STOP, SHOP—AND GO MALLING

Three decades ago shopping centers were rarities. Where they existed at all, they tended to be small. Today there are more than 23,000 of them, covering an average of 137,000 square feet each and annually ringing up $416 billion in retail sales. Once restricted to the suburbs, they are now cropping up in the hearts of cities like Washington, D.C., with its Victorian-style Georgetown Park *(left)*.

The secret of their success has perhaps as much to do with their entertainment value as it does with the convenience of having dozens of shops under one roof and a spot to park as well. They are airily designed, with wide corridors, open areas, plants and plenty of benches for the tired to rest their feet. And they offer a variety of diversions, from movie theaters, restaurants and skating rinks to arts, crafts and antique shows. They are places, as a new word has it, to go malling — to mosey, to see and be seen, to while away an hour or two among other human beings. Indeed, they have all but replaced Main Street as America's marketplace and Saturday hangout.

Teenagers love them and congregate in them, and many of the elderly have made of them a second home. Said one old-timer, likening the mall he and his friends frequent almost every day to the general store of the past: "Instead of sitting around the pot-bellied stove, we have various places where we cluster, and we visit."

Built on three levels around a skylit atrium whose main feature is an elaborate fountain, Georgetown Park in Washington, D.C., attracts hundreds of thousands of customers a year to its more than 80 stores and restaurants.

other users, from transportation and warehousing to advertising and accepting the customer's money in a retail store. An estimated one third to one half of the U.S. labor force is employed in some phase of marketing.

A substantial portion of the money spent on marketing goes to advertising. Advertising has been a fact of economic life since Babylonian merchants put up signs describing their wares 5,000 years ago. But no other economy has ever been as advertising-oriented as that of the U.S., where $60 billion were spent on advertisements annually in the 1980s. Studies indicate that the average American consumer is exposed to approximately 1,500 ads each day, and actually takes mental note of about 75 of these. By and large, Americans, including the many children who watch commercial television for hours on end, are fairly discriminating, even cynical, about most advertising, extracting whatever information they want from it and mentally thumbing their noses when confronted by oversell.

Like it or not, Americans are stuck with advertising, and have been since the middle of the 19th century, when factories started turning out more goods than could be sold by traditional, leisurely methods of marketing. For advertising is not simply the oil of the U.S. economic machine; it is the power that drives it. As an advertising textbook so candidly puts it: "The mass production of products and services requires constant selling pressure to keep consumption high."

American advertising has spread well beyond U.S. shores, as have various other services, earning foreign exchange that improves the country's balance of payments and thus its ability to buy desirable products from abroad.

Exportable services include not only obvious foreign-currency earners such as airlines, but various kinds of financial services and even the selling of hamburgers, as has been ably demonstrated by a man named Ray Kroc.

When Kroc founded McDonald's Hamburgers in 1955, he launched a new American service industry, the fast-food business. Today, fast-food providers like McDonald's and its proliferating competitors make inexpensive meals easily accessible to virtually all Americans. Fast-food hamburgers, pizzas, fried chicken and even Chinese egg rolls now amount to a $25-billion-a-year industry in the U.S.

In building his business, Kroc relied on clever mass-marketing and advertising techniques. While retaining ownership of some of the outlets, he sold franchises for about three in every four to local entrepreneurs, who built and then operated the restaurants. Kroc supplied the McDonald's name, methods, mass purchasing power in buying supplies, and nationwide advertising. In return, he received a percentage of each outlet's gross sales.

Kroc also applied the principles of standardization that were developed in mass production. Machines precut the hamburger to precisely 1.6 ounces of beef; computerized deep fryers ensure that each batch of French fries has the correct crispness; dispensers squeeze out identical dollops of ketchup. Although some Americans resent the homogenization of their culture that McDonald's represents, an estimated 4 percent of the U.S. population visits a McDonald's on any given day. There are now more than 5,500 McDonald's outlets in the U.S. — and another 1,200 in 29 foreign countries.

Perhaps the most fascinating indi-

cation of the service economy's growth is the fact that many services operate on behalf of other service industries. Consider the temporary-employment business, an eight-billion-dollar-a-year industry to which an estimated 70 percent of all American businesses turn annually, whenever they need extra help but do not wish to increase their permanent payrolls.

The founder of the temporary-help business was Russell Kelly, progenitor of the famous "Kelly girls." Kelly knew a lot about efficiency. As a fiscal-management analyst in the U.S. Army during World War II, he had established a centralized system for speeding up the payment of invoices and the delivery of food. A colleague noted that Kelly "moved food the way General Patton rolled his tanks."

In 1946 Kelly set up an office staffed by two young women and offered Detroit businesses help with their typing and clerical work. He intended to provide that help in his own office, but quickly found out that businesses preferred to have the work done on their premises. He began sending out his "Kelly girls" to fill in for absent secretaries or to augment the client's regular office staff during peak work periods.

Today, Kelly Services, Inc. employs more than 300,000 temporary workers, men as well as women, who operate from more than 500 branch offices in the United States and abroad. They fill more than 100 job classifications, from file clerk to computer programmer to product demonstrator to registered nurse. The range of specialties reflects the ever-broadening scope of service occupations in an economy whose success now depends on far more than the fertility of farmland or the speed of assembly lines. □

HARVEST OF GOOD LIVING

The growth of corporate agriculture does not worry Ben Dieterich, 30, who with his family and one hired hand farms 1,500 acres in central Texas. "The family farm is here to stay," he says. "A corporation couldn't make this farm pay; it takes too much overtime."

Dieterich labors from early morning to nightfall (and at harvest, several hours after dark), with enough modern equipment to stock a dealer's showroom — including three tractors, three cultivators and a $70,000 combine harvester. The high cost of machines plus the expense of seed, fertilizer and pesticides makes a farm like Dieterich's a capital-intensive, high-risk business. "It takes pretty near half a million dollars just to start," he observes, "and you could almost be wiped out in one bad year." To guard against that, he diversifies his acreage and effort between wheat, corn and cattle, while his wife, Lou Ann, cultivates a garden that feeds the family year round.

The Dieterichs must pay to lease most of the land they farm (they own 97 acres) and are paying off some $100,000 in short-term loans for operating capital. But despite the risks and the hard work, says Lou Ann, "farm life is the best life," and Ben agrees. "I don't think I could bear to do anything else," he says. "I love farming."

Behind the ranch-style house the Dieterichs designed for themselves, Lou Ann hangs out the family laundry (she has an electric dryer but likes the fresh smell of clothes that have been dried in sunshine). "On a farm with three boys," she says, "you have to wash every single day."

In May, a harvest month for winter wheat in Texas, Ben Dieterich shows sons Chris, 8, and Jason, 5, how he estimates the grain's moisture content. The crop will be ready to cut only when the sun has dried it sufficiently.

Chris Dieterich (in cap) and his younger brothers feed ground corn to a cow (foreground) and a Brahman bull. This unusually gentle bull is one of two the Dieterichs keep for breeding. Calves sired by Brahmans — descended from Indian stock — can withstand pests, disease and Texas heat.

Lou Ann boils plums to make jelly. She cans or freezes some 280 quarts of home-grown produce yearly.

Ben washes a truck loaned to him for being selected Texas' Outstanding Young Farmer.

86

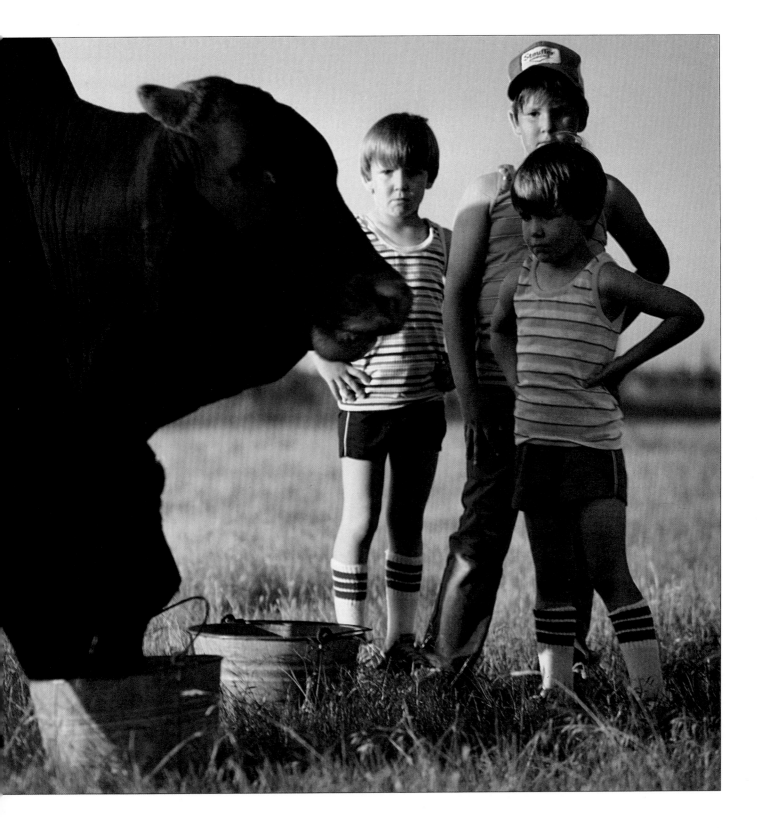

At his desk in the kitchen, Ben brings his accounts up to date. He does all the bookkeeping for the farm, having learned it on his own. The Texas-shaped mirror and other items on the wall memorialize his selection as an outstanding young farmer.

While hired hand José Rodríguez pumps diesel fuel into a tractor, Ben *(left)* performs some last-minute maintenance before the harvest. Ben keeps 1,000 gallons of fuel in tanks on the farm, and he and José do all repair work on the machinery.

From the comfort of his combine harvester's air-conditioned cab, Ben cuts a 22-foot-wide swath across one of his wheat fields. In a 12-hour day he can cover 100 acres in the machine, which cuts and threshes the grain, then spouts it into a hopper.

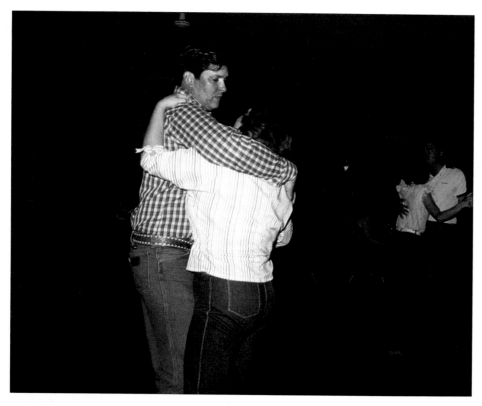

Stealing a few hours of relaxation
after a hard week of work, Ben and Lou
Ann slow-dance to country music
at the Melody Ranch, a nightclub in
Waco, 20 miles from the farm.
They go dancing about once a month.

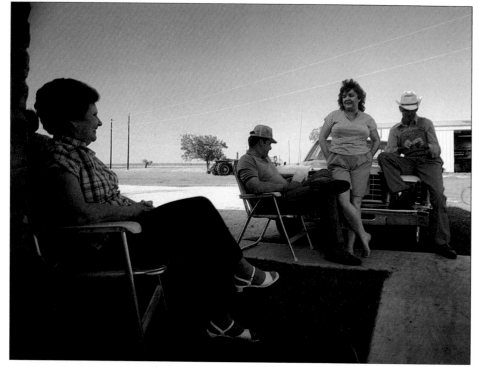

Ben's mother *(left)* and father *(right)*
join the Dieterichs for a lazy Sunday
afternoon on the farmhouse
driveway, which doubles as a patio.
Descended from a German farmer
who immigrated to Texas four
generations ago, Ben has some 200
relatives living within 20 miles.

Jason *(foreground)* and Brandon pedal through puddles, reveling in the wetness and cool air that follow a Texas plains thunderstorm. Behind Jason are the farm's big aluminum equipment shed and a wooden barn that is used for hay storage.

4

The archetypal artifacts of American popular culture are jukeboxes — coin-in-a-slot phonographs like this 1939 model — that once played music in 250,000 bars and cafés across the U.S.

ARTS WITH MASS APPEAL

The land that perfected mass production perhaps inevitably turned assembly-line techniques to the manufacture of mass culture — music, movies, television shows and other forms of entertainment. Many nations made films: Hollywood turned the production of movies into a gigantic industry, at one time the nation's fifth largest in terms of sales. There was an appetite for them. By 1926, scarcely 15 years after the release of the first full-length moving picture, 20,000 movie theaters had been built in the U.S. And by the late 1920s Hollywood was making 700 to 800 films annually.

So it was with music. In 1907, the heyday of sheet-music publishing, 42 songs sold a million or more copies each to customers who took them home to play on the parlor piano. When the phonograph replaced the family piano, record sales became a major American industry. In 1921 a hundred million discs were sold in the U.S.; by 1930, however, the figure had plummeted to six million a year.

The villain was radio — another technological advance that spawned a mass-culture industry. There were eight radio stations in 1920; nine years later there were 300. By the early 1930s a third of all U.S. homes had a radio, providing a potential audience of 60 million listeners for any one program.

Then along came television, and the hunger for entertainment via the small screen proved insatiable. By the mid-1980s nearly every American household — 83 million of them — had at least one television set. To serve the nation's viewers, more than 800 commercial stations had been established around the country, so many that 90 percent of the viewers could choose from among at least four channels. By the mid-1980s there were 4,800 cable TV systems catering to 23 million subscribers. And the average household had its set turned on an astonishing six hours and 48 minutes a day.

To keep images flickering nonstop on all those screens, the U.S. television industry was forced to produce many thousands of hours of entertainment in addition to news broadcasts and the rerunning of old movies. Between the mid-1960s and the mid-1980s the three major networks devoted an average of 1,438 prime-time hours each year to that most characteristic form of American television entertainment, the serial dramatic show. Such continued dramas — along with other American-made programs — have proved astonishingly popular abroad; by the mid-1980s U.S. television producers were exporting 300,000 hours' worth of programing to stations in more than 100 foreign countries. Critics in some of those nations have cried out at this "cultural imperialism," but their carping only underlines the enormous effect American popular arts have had around the globe.

America's cultural impact has not of course been confined to the masses. For a nation comparatively so young, the U.S. has cast up an impressive number of recognized masters throughout the arts. The stories and novels of Nathaniel Hawthorne, Herman Melville, Henry James, Edith Wharton and William Faulkner bear comparison with the finest fiction from anywhere. Painting has flourished in the works of the great portraitists John Singleton Copley and Thomas Eakins, the superb watercolors of Winslow Homer and the haunting, realistic canvases of Edward Hopper.

The post-World War II Abstract Expressionist school was the first American-born art movement to exert an international influence. Jackson Pollock, Robert Motherwell and Willem De Kooning became familiar names in art circles the world over. America has given the world great sculptors in Augustus Saint-Gaudens, Alexander Calder, David Smith and Louise Nevelson, and notable composers of classical music in Charles Ives and Aaron Copland.

Yet America's unique contribution to world culture is in the popular realm. Hollywood not only turned filmmaking into an industry, it also invented several sorts of movies — most notably Western and gangster dramas — that have attracted enormous attention worldwide. Starting from the European operetta, U.S. composers and librettists created an essentially new form of entertainment, the Broadway musical. When African and European musical traditions met in America, they combined to produce a musical expression like no other — jazz, and its outgrowths such as rock and roll.

Mass production of radios and innovations in advertising interacted in the late 1920s to bring forth another native entertainment form, daytime radio serials — better known as soap operas or

4

A metal "mobile" 86 feet across —
created by U.S. sculptor Alexander
Calder — pivots slowly in the National
Gallery in Washington, D.C. The
National, only one of America's
thousands of busy museums, hosts
five million visitors annually.

simply "soaps" because the sponsoring advertisers were generally selling cleansers. With the coming of television the soaps became visual and grew into a staple of daytime programing, and even invaded evening "prime time."

Many of the works turned out by Hollywood and other segments of the huge U.S. entertainment industry have been, despite a high gloss of professionalism, very low on the artistic scale. Yet in the hands of their most gifted creators, the popular arts have on occasion reached the level of high art. These creators, rather than fabricating homogenized products, have put their own ideas and feelings into their works. Instead of exploiting the public, they have tried to communicate with it and in doing so, have fashioned a surprising number of genuine masterpieces.

One of the greatest of these artists was that blend of suave elegance and musical genius named Duke Ellington. By all odds, he was during his lifetime the most distinguished writer of jazz music, and the most indefatigable. From his first piece in 1923 until his death, of cancer, in 1974, he composed or co-authored more than 1,500 original works, many of them — both joyful stomps and moody, poignant laments — summations of the essential nature of jazz and of the black experience in America. In company with a handful of gifted instrumentalists such as trumpeter Louis Armstrong and pianist Earl Hines, Ellington in the 1920s turned jazz from a mixture of popular and folk music into true art. He pioneered so inventively in musical sounds and forms that all subsequent jazz creators have been in his debt.

When Edward Kennedy Ellington was born, in 1899 in Washington, D.C., one of the musical precursors of jazz

was already gaining popularity. This was ragtime, a bouncy, lilting type of piano music derived from the quadrille and the march by black musicians in the Midwest ("ragtime" was a black term for "syncopation"). The most distinguished composer of rags was Scott Joplin, a Texan from a poor but musical family. In the year of Ellington's birth, Joplin published his first work, the "Maple Leaf Rag."

This tune, which sold 400,000 copies in sheet music, helped start a ragtime craze that spread from the Midwest to New Orleans, Baltimore, New York and Washington, as well as abroad. In Washington, while the young Ellington was growing up, a half dozen black ragtime pianists flourished and the future composer early absorbed ragtime's melodies and catchy syncopations — cross rhythms and polyrhythms that, as

musicologist Gunther Schuller maintains, American blacks had retained in their songs and chants from their African homelands.

Ellington grew up a pampered child — "my parents were very strict," he later joked, "about seeing that I got everything I wanted." His doting mother and father provided early piano instruction — with a teacher named, improbably enough, Mrs. Clinkscales — but the lessons did not prosper. "I missed more than I took," Ellington recalled, "because of my enthusiasm for playing ball."

He nevertheless picked up enough knowledge of the piano to begin playing at high-school parties. He picked up more tips on piano technique by watching the pianists who frequented a Washington poolroom, where they entertained the pool players. He also — and this was important for his development — heard the piano roll of James P. Johnson's "Carolina Shout" at a friend's house, and spent hours running this breakneck number at slow speed through the piano so that he could follow the great New York pianist's fingering.

Armed with the "Carolina Shout" as his featured piece, Ellington increasingly eschewed baseball for music. By the age of 18, the Duke — as he was called by then, for his elegant dress and bearing — was forming his own small bands and playing at a variety of social functions. So successful did the young musical entrepreneur become that by the time he was 20 he was supporting a wife and a baby son comfortably, and owned his own house and car.

Despite his hometown success, Ellington hankered after the excitement of New York. In 1922 he took the leap, traveling with two fellow musicians to

This starkly graceful combination of molded plywood and tubular metal is probably the best-known piece of 20th-century American furniture. Designed by Charles Eames in 1946, it has been manufactured in the thousands.

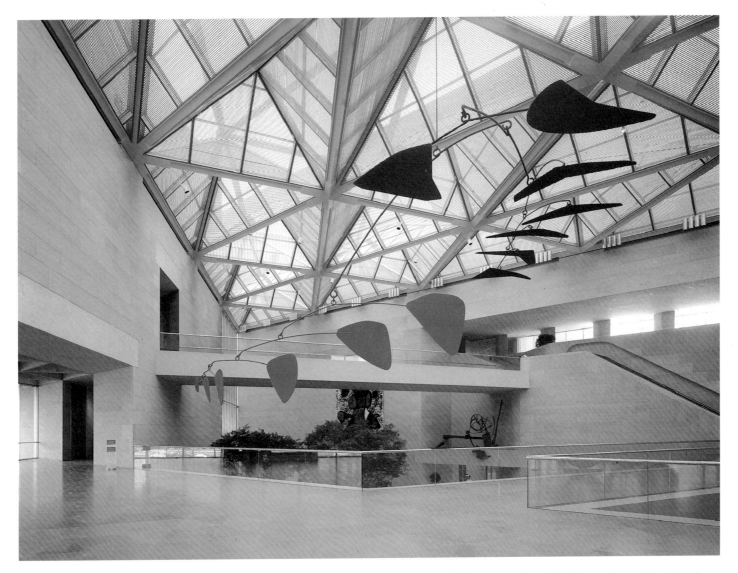

what was already the capital of the entertainment industry. But work was hard to find and at first they nearly starved. Eventually, they formed the "Washingtonians" and found a home in the Kentucky Club, a night spot at Broadway and 49th Street. There the band, now augmented by several new members, played for four years — to ever-increasing acclaim.

At the time, several sorts of jazz were heard in New York. There was the home-grown "Harlem Stride" piano music played by Ellington's idol, James P. Johnson, by Johnson's star pupil, a massive young man named Fats Waller, and by Willie "The Lion" Smith, whose unusual harmonies would permanently influence Ellington's own playing. Added to this were brassy sounds imported from New Orleans, where another kind of jazz had been born from a cross-fertilization of ragtime and the music of the Crescent City's many marching bands *(pages 106-113)*.

A five-piece group made up of white New Orleans musicians, the Original Dixieland Jazz Band, had brought a version of this music to New York as early as 1917. By the mid-1920s two superb instrumentalists, Sidney Bechet and Armstrong, had arrived in the city and added their own refined interpretations. Bechet, a clarinetist and soprano saxophonist, for some months blew his soaring, impassioned choruses as a member of Ellington's group at the Kentucky Club. Armstrong impressed every musician in town with the blazing, New Orleans-derived trumpet solos he played during the one year, 1924, that he spent with Fletcher

4

Henderson's orchestra at New York's Roseland Ballroom.

Then there were the blues, originating in the South and Southwest, and sung most memorably by the incomparable Bessie Smith. Her huge, resonant voice, one critic said, had "all the carrying quality (and some of the timbre) of a diesel locomotive horn," and her mesmeric and soulful laments, such as "Empty Bed Blues," defined what the blues could and should be.

All these stirring sounds invigorated Ellington's imagination and they were heard in the music his band was playing. At first, recalled Ellington's drummer, Sonny Greer, "Duke wasn't writing so much, but he would take the popular tunes and twist them" so that their small group sounded "like a big band, but soft and beautiful." Soon, however, the Duke was composing original material, some of it inspired by, and tailored to, the extraordinary muted, growling trumpet playing of Bubber Miley and the equally eerie growls and wails that Charlie Irvis could achieve on the trombone. The band's new sound was dubbed the "jungle style" and it remained Ellington's trademark through the 1920s.

Ellington really launched his career as a composer, however, when in 1927 his band began a five-year stay at the Cotton Club, then Harlem's flossiest night spot. Ellington was required to write both dance tunes and a variety of production numbers for the shows. He also enlarged the band from six to 11 pieces and, finding himself with an even more richly timbred, various and versatile aggregation than before, began to compose original numbers that would exploit its musical resources.

Part of Ellington's genius went into forming this superb orchestra, which,

in the words of photographer and writer Gordon Parks, could "unfold softly like a flower or explode like a bomb." Largely because it was the medium through which he expressed himself, the Duke kept his orchestra together for 50 years, with many of the key men staying on for most of those decades.

For them Ellington wrote his famous melodies — "Sophisticated Lady," "Mood Indigo," "Solitude," "Don't Get Around Much Any More" — and also what can only be called swinging concerti that evoke a train ride ("Daybreak Express") or the sounds of a noisy tenement ("Harlem Air Shaft"). In these and others, such as "Morning Glory," "Ko-Ko" and "Conga Brava," Elling-

ton's writing and the band's playing produced what critic Whitney Balliett has called "a rending, incredibly rich sound that is one of the delights of Western orchestral music."

Despite the exhaustions of nonstop composing and long trips with the orchestra — to every corner of the country and to many parts of Europe — Ellington remained always the same: unruffled, urbane, dressed with impeccable taste. He was especially admired by blacks as an entertainer who was always dignified. "Ellington never grinned," Gordon Parks remembered. "He smiled. Ellington never shuffled. He strode. It was 'Good afternoon ladies and gentlemen,' never 'How y'all doin'?' " To Parks and other young blacks, Ellington was "elegant, handsome and awe-inspiring."

The Duke was as spirited, witty and inventive in his speech as he was in his music. When someone remarked that his gifted assistant arranger and all-around collaborator Billy Strayhorn, whom the Duke called "Swee' Pea," was "Ellington's alter-ego," the Duke slyly protested. "Let's not go overboard. Pea is only my right arm, left foot, eyes, stomach, ears and soul, not my ego." His charm was such that he could tell a woman, "I knew you were here because the whole studio was suddenly aglow with a turquoise radiance" — and get away with it.

During the Swing Era of the 1930s and early 1940s, Ellington and his band were never as popular with the dancing public as the slicker, more musically predictable orchestras of Tommy Dorsey, Benny Goodman and Count Basie. Because he and his men were black, they were for many years not allowed to perform in many hotel ballrooms and other prestigious auditoriums. Asked about this, Ellington gave a characteristically wry answer: "I took the energy it takes to pout and wrote some blues."

But eventually the recognition the Duke deserved came his way. He was awarded at least 15 honorary doctoral degrees by U.S. colleges and universities, given the keys to 13 American cities as well as the Presidential Medal of Freedom, the nation's highest civilian award. But perhaps Ellington's ultimate reward was the pleasure he took in his own work — and in seeing others the world over enjoy it too.

The rhythms and sounds of ragtime and jazz strongly influenced the originators of the Broadway musical, another indigenous American creation,

and gave their shows much of their spark and appeal. It was no accident that one of the first songs written by a Manhattan singing waiter named Israel Baline — better known as Irving Berlin — was titled "Alexander's Ragtime Band," or that one of the first numbers George Gershwin wrote with his lyricist brother Ira began, "The real American folksong is a rag."

American musical comedies were the product in part of European operettas with their gossamer-thin plots and romantic music, and in part of such native-born entertainments as theatrical revues and vaudeville. The impresario Florenz Ziegfeld staged revues he called the *Follies* year after year and he was rivaled in the early 1920s by producer George White's *Scandals* and by Irving Berlin's *Music Box Revues*. In the mid-1920s the operetta and the theatrical revue coalesced in a new and delicious confection, the musical play.

Most of the earliest musicals had plots as thin as the airiest operetta. The Gershwins' first major success, *Oh, Kay!* (1926), was a bit of Prohibition-era nonsense about an impoverished English lord who sets out to restore the family fortunes by bootlegging liquor from his yacht to the shores of Long Island. But it was of course the songs that George and Ira hung on such shaky plot lines that enchanted the original audiences and still delight the listener today.

George's dazzlingly fertile musical imagination poured out several hundred such melodies. He also found time to write longer symphonic compositions such as his jazz-based *Rhapsody in Blue* and *Concerto in F,* as well as his wonderful opera, *Porgy and Bess.* Even before his tragically premature death at the age of 38 in 1937 of a brain tumor, Gershwin was hailed by some critics as

the greatest of all American composers.

Virtually all of the musicals of the 1920s and 1930s were giddily plotted excuses for good songs, sprightly dance numbers, a bit of romance and some comedy routines. But then in December, 1927, a musical arrived on Broadway that would help shatter this tradition. It was *Show Boat,* with music by Jerome Kern and lyrics by Oscar Hammerstein II. When the curtains parted on opening night, there were no giddy singing-and-dancing chorines, but a group of black dock workers soulfully lamenting the drudgery of lifting back-breaking bales of cotton. As the story unfolded, it became clear that the songs were not simply charming interludes. Hammerstein's lyrics advanced the plot and explained character, while Kern's music reinforced the mood. This new element of seriousness and unification of song and story captured theatergoers' imaginations. *Show Boat* became such a hit that on completion of its New York run, it toured the country for seven months.

Another major breakthrough occurred in 1940 with Richard Rodgers and Lorenz Hart's *Pal Joey.* The musical was something of an anti-romance; the hero was a callous con man and gigolo. But this did not make the team's songs any less memorable or delightful. Hart was one of the greatest masters of comic rhyme since Lord Byron wrote *Don Juan,* and *Pal Joey* is full of them. Lamenting her infatuation with the faithless Joey, the play's heroine opines that she is "wild again! / Beguiled again! / A simpering, whimpering child again!" Then she adds that "A pill he is, / But still he is / All mine and I'll keep him until he is / Bewitched, bothered, and bewildered / Like me!"

After that show, musicals gained a

4

new maturity, a new coordination between libretto, tunes, lyrics and even ballet-like dance numbers that also served to help tell the story. One of the masters of the new musical was Cole Porter, who, like Berlin, wrote the lyrics for his own songs. In his most insouciant and sophisticated show, *Kiss Me Kate,* virtually every song contributes directly to furthering the plot or giving new depth to the characters.

Words and music are also tightly tied to the story of Frank Loesser's *Guys and Dolls* and Berlin's *Annie Get Your Gun.* But perhaps the masterpieces of the genre are *My Fair Lady,* the superb musical version of George Bernard Shaw's play *Pygmalion,* by Alan Jay Lerner and Frederick Loewe; and *Oklahoma!* and *South Pacific,* two works by Richard Rodgers and Oscar Hammerstein II. In them all, music and words, plot and dance, setting and action are so completely married to each other that something close to a new and utterly beguiling form of theatrical art became the result.

Long before this post-World War II apotheosis of the musical took place, while jazz and other forms of 20th century popular music were in their infancy, another popular art to which the U.S. made crucial and original contributions was coming of age: the movies. For 40 years, beginning in about 1920, the movies were the dominant form of mass entertainment in America. Indeed, for millions of Americans, they were the only form of dramatic entertainment. So pervasive, so powerful was the effect of movies on the American public that they did not so much mirror life, as life mirrored the movies. When in the romantic comedy *It Happened One Night* Clark Gable undressed to reveal he wore no undershirt, the

sales of such garments plummeted across the nation.

For all practical purposes, the American movie was born in 1903 in Thomas A. Edison's laboratories in New Jersey, where a cameraman named Edwin Porter created *The Great Train Robbery,* an eight-minute film that electrified the public and also introduced several motifs that would characterize many American movies to come. It was a Western, it was populated by easily recognized good guys and bad, and it introduced the speed and suspense of the chase scene.

The next great step was taken in 1915 when a onetime actor named David Wark Griffith produced his epic *Birth of a Nation,* which chronicled the Civil War era and the rise of the Ku Klux Klan during the Reconstruction period. Lasting an unheard-of three hours, Griffith's drama revolutionized filmmaking around the world. "It established," said one film historian, "the immense power of the medium to produce extended emotional and psychological effects."

It was in the realm of film comedy, however, that early American moviemakers truly led the world. The first and still-unchallenged king of comedy was a frustrated opera singer from East Berlin, Connecticut, named Mack Sennett, who, although he mass-produced his two-reel farces, achieved in many of them a sublime poetry of comic chaos.

Beginning in 1909, Sennett scoured America's circuses and burlesque and vaudeville houses for the best and broadest slapstick comedians he could find. He formed them into a repertory company that featured the Keystone Kops, seven of the most insanely incompetent policemen ever seen on earth. The Kops inevitably became em-

ADORED RELICS OF ELVIS

In the decades after World War II, a musical mania called rock and roll — a thumping, shouting, twanging outgrowth of jazz — swept the U.S. and then the world. The unquestioned monarch of rock — at least until England's Beatles adapted the music — was a former truck driver named Elvis Presley. So adored was Elvis by his millions of fans that, since his death of a heart attack at the age of 42 in 1977, such artifacts as his automobiles have been treasured with almost religious awe.

Rock and roll was created by black musicians in the late 1930s, and it appealed almost exclusively to a black audience — until Elvis. Born in Tupelo, Mississippi, and raised in Memphis, Tennessee, he borrowed the rhythmic drive and vocal intonations of the largely Southern black rockers, popularizing the music and vastly broadening its audience. His first major record, "Heartbreak Hotel," sold three million copies. Within two years Presley had grossed $100 million. By 1968, 200 million of his discs had sold and he had appeared in 29 movies — at an average fee of $850,000 each.

A good measure of Presley's huge popularity could be attributed to the wild physical gyrations — he was dubbed "Elvis the Pelvis" — that accompanied his singing. To his teen-age fans, his movements and rich voice spoke of sex, independence and revolt against authority. Yet Elvis appears to have been an ill-adjusted and fearful man who at the height of his fame — and despite his enormous wealth — became a near-recluse in his Memphis mansion, where he retreated further into the drug use that seems to have hastened his premature death.

A plaster portrait of Presley *(right)*, one of the millions of Elvis images made during his lifetime, stares from a shop window. It emphasizes the hooded eyes and brooding look that entranced his female fans.

The interior of Presley's favorite Cadillac *(below)* has electric shoe-shining gear, a record player, a television set and a make-up mirror — appurtenances mostly finished in 24-carat gold plate. The car is preserved in a museum in Nashville, Tennessee, center for another native American musical form, country and western.

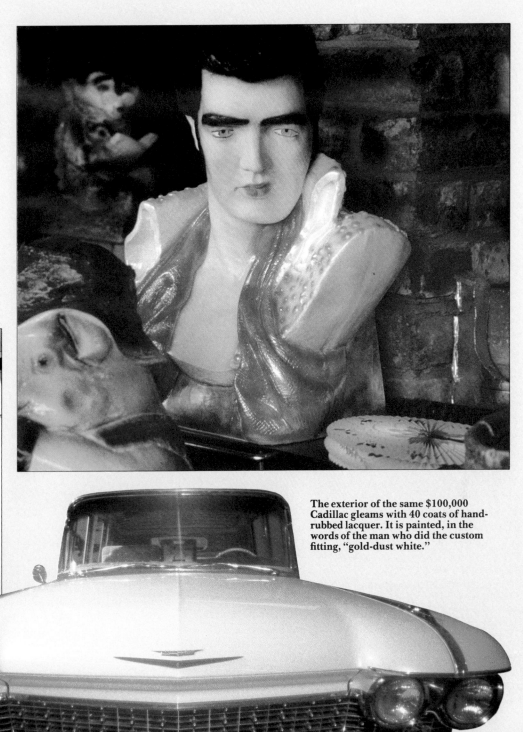

The exterior of the same $100,000 Cadillac gleams with 40 coats of hand-rubbed lacquer. It is painted, in the words of the man who did the custom fitting, "gold-dust white."

broiled with some equally daffy male civilians and with Sennett's troupe of Bathing Beauties, a gaggle of hearty young women in disconcerting knee-length swimsuits. "All these people," wrote James Agee, the critic and film writer *(The African Queen)*, "zipped and caromed about the pristine world of the screen as jazzily as a convention of water bugs. Words can hardly describe how energetically they collided and bounced apart, meeting in full gallop around the corner of a house; how hard and how often they fell on their backsides; or with what fantastically adroit clumsiness they got themselves fouled up in folding ladders, garden hoses, tethered animals and each other's headlong cross-purposes."

Sennett perfected the chase sequence, and virtually all of his farces end with the Kops and others in pell-mell pursuit of some poor fleeing scapegoat who has aroused their ire. Sennett's chases built up "such a majestic trajectory of pure anarchic motion," Agee wrote, "that bathing girls, cops, comics, dogs, cats, babies, automobiles, locomotives, innocent bystanders, sometimes what seemed like a whole city, an entire civilization, were hauled along head over heels in the wake of that energy like dry leaves following an express train."

Sennett claimed to have originated the technique of speeding up the action of silent comedies by cranking the camera too slowly. When the film was shown by a normal-speed projector, the action became faster and fizzier than real life. He also fostered the development of that archetypal comic device, the custard pie in the face.

The apex of the art was reached, however, in a two-reeler by Sennett's rival, Hal Roach, featuring the comic team of Stan Laurel and Oliver Hardy. Early in the film a bakery truck is parked in the middle of a street scene, providing limitless ammunition for the battle to come. Laurel and Hardy begin the pie throwing, of course, but ultimately a dozen passersby become involved; the finale is a custard Armageddon with dozens, hundreds, of pies flying through the air.

Sennett and Roach and other makers of Hollywood comedy did not strive consciously for artistic form. Their consuming aim was simply to delight movie audiences by reducing them to helpless laughter. But they achieved on occasion a pure and innocent perfection of comic art, piling one hilarious device upon another to reach a crescendo of frenzied motion.

Another of Sennett's contributions to comedy was to nurture the talents of a pair of comedians who would raise silent comedy to new levels of artistry, Charles Chaplin and Buster Keaton. An English music-hall comedian who made 30 films for Sennett before going on his own, Chaplin early created his immortal Tramp. Dressed in absurdly ill-fitting clothes — oversized pants and undersized jacket and derby — Chaplin's waif became the eternal victim of manic fold-out beds, whirling revolving doors and, ultimately, modern mechanical society as a whole. The figure of the Tramp became as familiar around the world as Mickey Mouse *(opposite)* and equally loved.

In his fine longer films such as *City Lights* and *The Gold Rush,* Chaplin could combine pathos — always inherent in the Tramp figure — and even tragedy with his inspired slapstick. In *City Lights* the Tramp has somehow found the money to help a blind flower girl have an operation that restores her sight.

She has imagined her benefactor as princely, not as an absurd semi-outcast. The Tramp for his part has never realized his own inadequacies. Then, no longer blind, she sees the Tramp for the first time. As Agee describes the scene: "She recognizes who he must be by his shy, confident, shining joy as he comes silently toward her. And he recognizes himself, for the first time, through the terrible changes in her face." It is a scene, Agee concludes, that can "shrivel the heart to see, and it is the greatest piece of acting and the highest moment in movies."

Keaton's comedy was also refined and subtle, but in a different way. After playing in several Keystone efforts, he produced on his own a sequence of two dozen or so superb films that include some of the most deft and preposterous — but also strangely moving — comic sequences ever invented.

Keaton, born in 1895, was already playing the part of a human volleyball in his parents' rough-and-tumble vaudeville act at the age of three and a half. Part of the comedy came from the boy's ability to hurtle about the stage without changing expression; ever after, he was "The Great Stone Face," meeting all crises with a mask as fixed and haunting as an old daguerreotype.

When he came to make his own movies in 1920, Keaton was the past master of the pratfall and every other gesture in the vocabulary of silent comedy. He went on to elaborate and refine them with unparalleled inventiveness. His *Cops* is one long chase, but here Keaton is pursued not by half a dozen incompetent Keystoners, but by an entire metropolitan police force with hundreds of cops snatching at his coattails. In *Sherlock Jr.* he engineers a superb variant on the chase sequence, wheeling dizzily

AN EMPIRE BUILT BY A MOUSE

Mickey and Pluto confer eye-to-eye in *The Pointer*, a 1939 cartoon about hunting.

One of this century's most celebrated personalities has been that amiable rodent, Mickey Mouse, created by Walter Elias Disney. The huge company Disney built on Mickey's fame must be judged the leading purveyor of mass entertainment in U.S. history.

Disney's early years gave little promise of his later achievements. He dropped out of school in the ninth grade to become a commercial artist in Kansas City, but success eluded him. When he went to Hollywood in 1923 to try making animated cartoons, all he took with him were drawing skills and the memory of a friendly mouse that had shared his studio. After another five hungry years, Disney remembered his furry companion and made him the hero of a crude cartoon called *Steamboat Willie*.

Mickey was an instant hit, as were the playmates Disney soon gave him, such as the irascible Donald Duck and the faithful hound Pluto. When the costs of making short cartoons rose sharply and reduced profits, he cannily began producing high-profit feature-length animated films. The first, *Snow White*, grossed eight million dollars on its initial release in 1937, earning more than any other film up to that date. Other productions were almost as profitable. By the mid-1950s Disney had made 657 films, seen by an estimated one billion people.

And he was far from through. During the 1950s he began turning out adventure films with live actors as well as nature films such as *The Living Desert* — which cost $300,000 and took in five million dollars worldwide. In addition, before his death in 1966 Disney created two successful amusement parks, Disneyland in California and Disney World in Florida.

Disney's friends and associates have agreed that his success arose from his ceaseless energy and his ability to retain the outlook of a child. He looked at the world, said artist Salvador Dali, "with uncontaminated wonder." Disney had his own view of the matter: "We're selling corn, and I like corn."

through rush-hour traffic on the handlebars of a motorcycle, unaware that the driver has been left behind.

He was also a master at twisting impossible situations. As an early Christian martyr thrown into a lion's den, he plays Androcles and removes a thorn from the lion's paw. Then, in a lovely parody of a manicurist's routine, he buffs the complaisant beast's claws.

Through all his trials Keaton remained undefeated. Chaplin wrung pathos from the defeats and humiliations suffered by his Tramp, but in Keaton's films there is no sentimentality. Behind that stoic mask there is always an unconquerable will to survive, even to triumph.

While Keaton, Chaplin and their fellow masters of silent comedy were developing and refining their art, other U.S. filmmakers were inventing and elaborating other uniquely American types of movies — the Western, then the gangster epic and later, after the coming of sound to pictures, the filmed musical comedy. Of them all, the most enduringly popular, both in the United States and around the world, has been the Western. To many of the world's moviegoers, America *is* the West as shown in these films, a huge, empty land across which desperadoes, bands of whooping Indians and lone gunfighters eternally gallop.

The U.S. film industry began to make Westerns, right from the start. The pioneering director D. W. Griffith filmed a number of short Westerns, starting as early as 1908. Since then, so many have been produced that an estimated one fourth of all films ever made in the U.S. have been Westerns.

Their universal and lasting appeal has certainly been partly due to the movies' sheer excitement — the gun play, the breakneck horseback pursuits, the careening stagecoaches under attack by Indians or outlaws. But there is also the nostalgia they bring for what seems a better, simpler time. The date in Westerns is always about 1870; the dramas are set in a pristine world, unfouled by cities and beyond the trammels of civilization. It is a world where right and wrong, the good guys and the bad, are usually clearly identified.

Still another reason the public has loved Westerns is their ritualistic qual-ity, their familiar settings and virtually identical casts of characters. The usual scene is a dusty frontier town with a bank, sheriff's office and saloon and dance hall. Equally familiar are the town's inhabitants, who include, in one critic's list, "the sheriff, the doctor, the prostitute, the telegrapher, the saloon keeper, and the quiet mysterious stranger who wanders in and may be the fastest gun alive." The moviegoer also recognizes "the hired killer, the ranching baron, the cardsharp, and the itin-erant notion-vendor" and understands "the rituals of the posse, the hanging party, the cavalry rescue" and especially "the shoot-out on the main street."

The focus of the drama is, of course, the "mysterious stranger," the gunfighter, the Westerner himself. It is in him — the furious action and the rituals aside — that the main appeal of the Western film resides. Some of the attractions of this hero are obvious: He is tall, self-contained to the point of silence, rides a horse faultlessly, employs his pistols only reluctantly but then better than anyone else — and, as critic Robert Warshow has noted, "can keep his countenance in the face of death."

His appeal is even deeper. Unlike the average man or woman, he does not seem to need to make a living, much less "get ahead" in the world. If he is acting as the town sheriff, he gets paid, but no amount of money could be sufficient recompense for the risks he takes. When asked why he must defy seemingly certain death to defeat the villains, he is likely to explain simply that he "has to do it."

In the final analysis, what the hero must perform is a self-assigned duty. What he defends, as Warshow has put it, is "the purity of his own image — in fact, his honor." In short, Western movies and their heroes have probably derived much of their enormous appeal from the fact that they satisfy deep, unspoken desires in their audiences — a longing to believe that they too could show such courage under pressure, that worldly success is not after all the most important thing in life, that the concept of personal honor still has validity and meaning.

So popular is the genre that film-makers in such unlikely places as Japan, Germany, India, Italy and even the So-

Ginger Rogers and Fred Astaire, the most brilliant dance team to grace that peculiarly American art form, the film musical, whirl through one of their celebrated numbers, "The Yam," in the 1938 movie *Carefree*. The duo made 10 movies together.

viet Union have made their own Westerns. At their worst these films have been mere pastiches of the original. And yet they have been amazingly profitable. If imitation is the sincerest form of flattery, nothing could more dramatically demonstrate the vast appeal of this peculiarly American form of film drama than these foreign rehashes of the genre.

While European directors and producers kept on making their own Westerns, Hollywood's production of Western films — and other sorts of movies as well — slowed to a crawl under the impact of that great post-World War II revolution in the entertainment industry, television. In 1947, movie attendance in the U.S. averaged 90 million a week. Ten years later this was cut in half. Meanwhile the number of television sets shot from 16,000 in 1947 to 33

million in 1955 and 150 million by the mid-1980s, with more than 340 million elsewhere around the world.

The Western formula proved its perennial appeal in the new medium; a dozen of television's most popular dramatic shows were Westerns. Television, with its all-consuming appetite, also usurped and adapted other forms of entertainment. One was that uniquely American type of radio drama, the soap opera, which had been entrancing millions of housewives and other devotees weekday afternoons since the invention of the soaps in the late 1920s.

Detailing the adventures of all manner of imaginary characters, from small-town folk to big-city theater people, the daily 15-minute radio dramas followed a formula best described by humorist James Thurber. "A soap opera is a kind of sandwich," Thurber

wrote. "Between thick slices of advertising spread twelve minutes of dialogue, add predicament, villainy, and female suffering in equal measure, throw in a dash of nobility, sprinkle with tears, season with organ music, cover with a rich announcer sauce, and serve five times a week."

Considering the predictability of the formula, it is not surprising that soap operas seldom if ever reached even the lowest level of artistic value, but their production established new records for dramatic mass manufacture. Among the originators of the soap opera were a Chicago husband-and-wife team, Frank and Anne Hummert, who for a time tapped out thousands of words each week to keep their initial shows supplied with plots and dialogue. Soon, however, the Hummerts formed a corporation and hired a stable of "dialoguers" (in the trade's jargon) to turn out episodes at $125 a week. At one time in the mid-1930s the Hummerts had 67 shows on the air each week, worth nine million dollars in advertisers' money per year. As early as 1938 their serials had totaled five million words — about 55 full-length novels.

The all-time champion at producing scripts for the radio soaps appears to have been a onetime Chicago newspaperman named Robert Douglas Hardy Andrews, who was one of the first writers hired by the Hummerts. A six-foot-tall, 200-pound man with strong wrists and an apparently indestructible typewriter, Andrews quickly hit his stride, turning out five 15-minute scripts a day. Fueled daily by 40 cups of coffee, he averaged for some years 100,000 words per week and on one occasion, when an unusual number of scripts were required in a special hurry, produced 32,000 words in 20 hours.

The soap opera architect and writer with the greatest staying power, however, was Irna Phillips, an Ohio schoolteacher who in 1930, at the age of 28, went to Chicago and got herself a job dialoguing the early episodes of a soap called *Today's Children*. Within a few years Irna Phillips had become the undisputed Queen of the Soaps and she remained so for 40 years, until her death in 1973. She invented and wrote several of the most popular of all the serials, including *The Guiding Light* and *As the World Turns*. At her peak in the mid-1930s she was regularly turning out 60,000 words per week and earning a handsome $250,000 a year or more — in pre-World War II dollars.

Irna Phillips' own interests and anxieties influenced the content of her serials and, because they proved popular, many other soaps as well. Her

The cast of the television hit *M*A*S*H* gathers around Alan Alda *(standing, third from left)*, who acted in every episode and directed and wrote some of the best. The show, which lasted longer than the Korean War it dramatized, was nominated for 99 of television's Emmy Awards and won 14.

memories of her small-town, family-oriented childhood encouraged her to put the challenges and troubles of everyday family life at the center of most of her creations. She was haunted by the fear of illness and fascinated by doctors. As a result her characters, and those of her many followers, were frequently afflicted by bizarre and terrible diseases, and were tended to by legions of glamorous M.D.s.

When television came along, a number of Phillips' soaps easily made the transition to being seen as well as heard. For a time in the mid-1970s her *As the World Turns,* by then carried on by her most successful disciple, Agnes Nixon, was among the most popular of all TV shows and Nixon's own *Search for Tomorrow* ranked as the longest-running show of any sort being shown on television.

By the late 1970s the soaps were having a further impact on television scheduling and on the viewing habits of millions that Irna Phillips perhaps never foresaw. The essential Phillipsian formula — the tribulations of a family continued with many variations week after week — had been adapted to evening, or "prime-time," dramas.

The most popular of these hour-long, once-a-week serial epics was *Dallas,* a riveting saga of lust and greed among the members of a Texas oil family. By the early 1980s the villainies of the ruthless antihero, J. R. Ewing, had become so irresistible that 40 million Americans were watching the show every week. It proved so popular in other parts of the world that it was being exported to 57 countries; for a time the rage for *Dallas* reached such proportions in England that 30 million people, more than half the population, tuned in for key episodes.

Television gave new life and vibrancy not only to soap operas, but also to the comedy programs that had been a staple of radio. The most popular was a show featuring a tall, red-headed actress who had played a number of wise-cracking parts in movies, Lucille Ball.

In 1951 Ball and her then-husband, a Cuban-born bandleader named Desi Arnaz, decided to find out what this new medium of television was all about. The Columbia Broadcasting System had asked her to come up with a comedy show that would be similar to one she had done on radio called *My Favorite Husband.* Ball and Arnaz concocted a story about a dizzy but endearing redhead who was married — of course — to a Cuban bandleader. Borrowing $5,000, they rented a California film studio, hired a cameraman and made the pilot show themselves.

The result was *I Love Lucy.* At the end of its first six months it was drawing the largest-ever TV audience and within two years Ball and Arnaz signed a contract for eight million dollars to continue producing and acting in it.

The success of *I Love Lucy* and its sequel, *The Lucy Show,* was its uncanny ability to adapt the formats of earlier radio comedy programs to television, and its charm was largely the result of Ball's combining this comedy with slapstick of a sort, including custard pies, that dated back to silent comedy. In *I Love Lucy,* the characters were faced each week with a problem that would intensify and ultimately get out of control until a rather improbable solution occurred. But despite the broad and outlandish comedy, Lucy remained a wholly sympathetic figure. The show went on and on, its popularity undimmed after 20 years. It has been dubbed into dozens of languages.

I Love Lucy gave rise to a wealth — some might say a plague — of similar comedies on television, a genre that soon gained the name of "situation comedy," or "sitcom." Few have had anything like the zip and sizzle of the Lucy shows. But a few have managed to portray characters recognizable as real people, and one or two have reached, improbably, something that could be called art, combining with their comedy a sense of reality and an appreciation of the complexity of human life.

The most compelling of these sitcoms seemed at first an unlikely candidate indeed. It was about a U.S. Army surgical unit during the Korean War — a group of doctors and nurses doing a grim job in a war-smashed corner of the earth. Yet *M*A*S*H* became a signpost of what television at its best could be. Despite the rapid-fire quips of the surgeons Hawkeye and Trapper John — and *M*A*S*H* could be very funny — it did not gloss over the horrors of war, and all of the characters, as week after week of the show went on, came to have unsuspected depths, unforeseen strengths and unexpected vulnerabilities. It became, as one critic mourning its last show in 1983 put it, "the most intelligent, passionate, imaginative and fiercely funny comedy series in the history of U.S. television."

As so often in matters of popular culture, the importance of an achievement can be measured in numbers. When *M*A*S*H* finally went off the air after 11 years and 251 episodes, the rate for a 30-second commercial had climbed to the stunning figure of $200,000. But *M*A*S*H* was able to tap the pocketbooks of advertisers only because it had touched something important in the makeup of its viewers — very possibly their hearts. □

Fans applaud the Humphrey brothers' band, one of four rotating groups that nightly draw crowds of jazz lovers to Preservation Hall in the French Quarter

SOUND OF THE CITY'S SOUL

Jazz emerged in New Orleans at the dawn of this century, and within a few decades it had spread around the world. But this uniquely American art form never really left home; it is still ingrained in the soul of the city. Jazz bursts from the doorways of Bourbon Street bars, pours from radios, enlivens parades, ennobles funerals. An estimated half of the 1,600 members of the local musicians' union are jazzmen, an impressive percentage in a city that embraces all kinds of music, from rock to symphonic.

And the city embraces all shades of jazz, too, from the slickly commercial to the avant-garde. But there is plenty of the purely traditional kind. Its practitioners include the combos at Preservation Hall (average age, 70-plus) and the schoolchildren learning their licks from men who studied with the pupils of such greats as Lorenzo Tio Jr.,"Big Eye" Louis Nelson, Alphonse Picou, Peter Bocage and George Baquet. Gaps in the ranks are quickly filled by eager young players carrying on a tradition now four generations old.

Night spots lining Bourbon Street blaze with light and pulse with sound. Here, on a corner of St. Peter Street, the Maison Bourbon proclaims its dedication to preserving jazz.

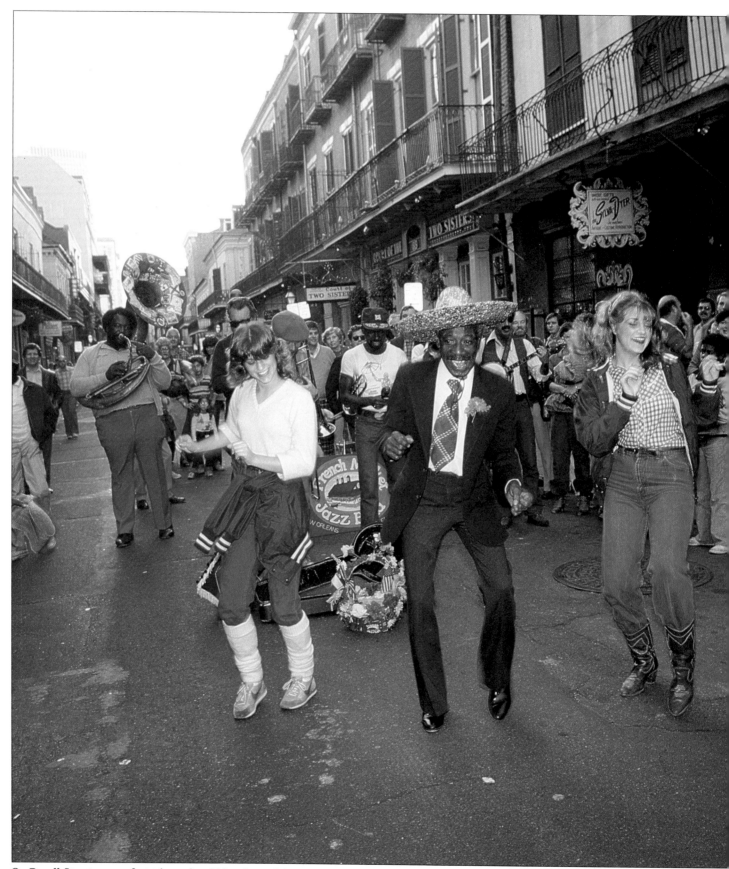

On Royall Street, young feet trip to the oldtime beat of the French Market Jazz Band. The front man's sombrero does double duty as collection plate.

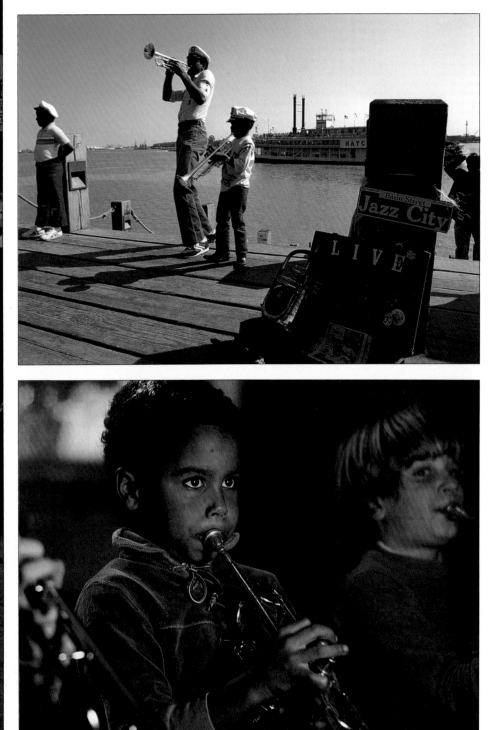

Jazz musician Charles Beasley and his son, aged five, stage a riverside trumpet duet. The Mississippi stern-wheeler behind them recalls days when such craft first carried jazz north.

New Orleans children take to jazz at an early age. These youngsters are playing at McDonogh School No. 15, where jazz is taught as a regular part of the music curriculum.

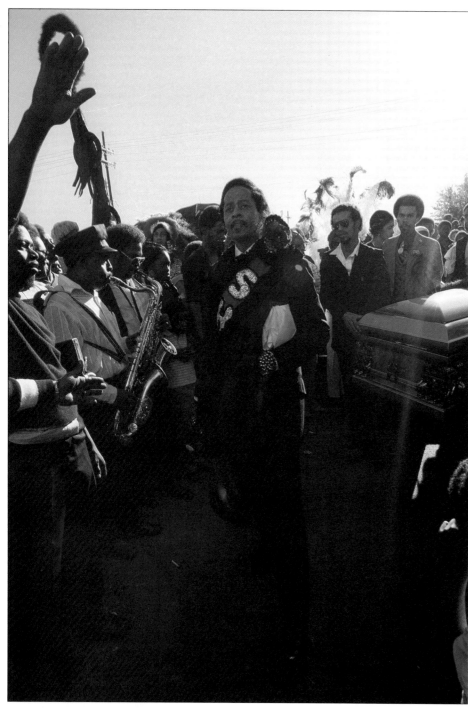

By a New Orleans custom older than the century, a marching band plays solemn music at the outset of a funeral procession. A member of a fraternal order leads the way in sequined sash and gloves, his white-plumed fan beneath his arm.

With whistle blasts and fan flourishes, a "captain" calls the tunes on the way back from the burial. The pace quickens to the beat of numbers like "Didn't He Ramble," and spectators form a joyous, dancing "second line" right behind the band.

Preston Jackson plays alone in the
courtyard of his Orleans Street home.
Born in 1902, he left New Orleans
at 15, played with various legendary
jazz figures and in the mid-1970s
revisited and fell under the spell of his
native city, where he remained,
because "I began to like what I saw."

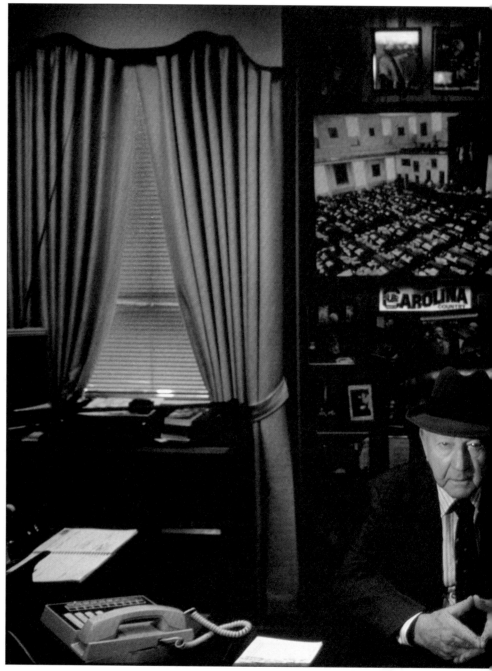

Assemblyman Solomon Blatt ponders a
point in his law office in Barnwell,
South Carolina. Most state assemblies
meet only one month a year, but
legislators like Blatt must contend with
demands from voters the year round.

THE POWER STRUCTURE

When an American speaks of "the system," he or she is probably discussing politics and is about to unload a complaint. "The system" is conversational shorthand for the forces, official and unofficial, that run the United States, whether at the local, the state or the national level.

Political power, vested by the Constitution in the people, derives in practice from the interaction of these forces and the constituencies they represent. In some instances the constituency may be the voters of a town or a congressional district. In others it might be a special-interest group: a labor union or a corporation or a local civic organization made up of homeowners who do not want a sewage-treatment plant built in their neighborhood.

The system, most Americans will readily avow, is far from perfect and often somewhat less than democratic. But in its own lumbering and cumbersome way, it usually gets the job done. That the system is imperfect and that it works anyway, often surprisingly well, may be the only two sweeping statements about it that would enjoy the concurrence of almost all Americans. Almost anything else that one might say — about who constitutes the U.S. power structure, about how and why it functions, about the nature of its major shortcomings — can be expected to meet substantial disagreement from one quarter or another.

The basic framework and processes of the federal government *(page 118)* are clearly delineated in the Constitution, and the structures of state and local governments are similar to the federal model. However, only school-children or the most naïve of adult Americans would contend that the nation (or any particular state or town in it) is run solely by elected and duly appointed officials performing their Constitutionally defined roles and keeping the best interests of the whole electorate always uppermost in their minds. Most people take it for granted that a multitude of other individuals and institutions — publicly recognized or shadowy, selfish or altruistic, righteous or nefarious — continually affect the course of government.

Consider, for instance, the news media. Those who are part of this institution — reporters, editors, television newscasters, owners of newspapers — generally believe that they have a special role in the system. They consider themselves the watchdogs of society, the protectors of the public's right to know what is going on, not only in government but also in private enterprises whose actions affect the public. But many Americans believe that the news media have arrogated more power to themselves than the Constitution meant them to have and therefore have too much of a hold on the public mind.

So it goes with other elements of the power structure. Environmentalists say that industrial corporations exert more

5

than their proper share of influence on government and jeopardize the nation's health by polluting air and water. Corporations allege that labor unions damage the economy by demanding exorbitant wages. Labor unions contend that environmentalists care more about recreation for the well-to-do than about jobs for workers. Some civil libertarians say that churches are too powerful and that they contrive to impose private morals on public law. And millions of Americans — like other people the world over — seem to believe that a vague entity identified as "they" controls everything. "They're raising prices again. . . . They're too soft on criminals. . . . They're getting us into another war."

Disputes about the nature of the U.S. power structure extend into expert circles. Some sociologists and political scientists hold that America has an oligarchical, even elitist, system, with power — be it at the local, state or national level — firmly in the grasp of a relative few. According to this theory, most of the important decisions about public policy are made by the elite, and only the details are worked out in open debate. Other scholars of society and politics take a pluralist view, saying that the system truly does accommodate the nation's multiplicity of wide-ranging interest groups, that it responds to shifting coalitions as they come together, achieve their purposes and then dissolve once again.

The majority of Americans would probably say that the pluralist version comes closer to the truth, although elites certainly are part of the U.S. power structure. In many a small community, leading citizens gather in the local coffee shop to thrash out issues privately before they meet in their official roles as members of the school board or city council to vote publicly on those same issues. Similarly, persons of substance in larger cities frequently find it more convenient, and more rewarding, to impart their views quietly to a mayor or governor, congressional representative or newspaper publisher while lunching at an exclusive club — such as the Pacific Union in San Francisco, the Somerset in Boston, or the Century in

New York — than to declare their aims to the public in an open forum.

But because the electorate can always use its votes to "turn the rascals out," in the words of an old American reformist battle cry, no elite can long maintain control of a city or state unless the government is satisfying the people. Sometimes the people are content as long as government is honest or at least has the appearance of honesty. In other instances, they appear to care less about honesty in government than about whether that government serves them in direct, tangible ways.

Such was long the case in Chicago, where the most important elite was the powerful Democratic party machine that ran the city and rewarded those who brought in the votes with lucrative patronage jobs. Honesty in political matters was never Chicago's long suit. Party workers have been known to vote tombstones — that is, to assist their candidates into office by casting ballots in the names of citizens who were in fact dead. But as long as the machine dispensed government jobs and contracts to faithful supporters and helped citizens to deal with the bureaucracy, it maintained tight control of the city. "Over at my headquarters," one long-time Chicago city council member explained to a reporter, "I've got lawyers, corporation counsel, an administrative assistant. You've got a legal matter? We turn it over to the lawyers. Free of charge. You've got a state matter? We've got a state representative in my organization. You've got a county matter? We've got a county commissioner. It doesn't matter what comes up. We give them service."

Apparently the machine did not give enough service to a growing number of black voters, who in 1983 helped elect

Crazy dress — like this delegate's hat — is *de rigueur* at political conventions, which are held every four years. Taking their carnival spirit into account, President Harry S. Truman could still say, "I do not know a better method for choosing a presidential nominee."

Chicago's first black mayor. He too was a Democrat, but the interests of his supporters did not mesh with those of the old machine, which managed to keep a majority in the city council. The ensuing power struggle within the municipal government made it clear that Chicago politics would never be the same again, that the old bosses would at the very least have to share their control of the city, if not yield it altogether.

At the national level, of course, the system is more complex. Many more interest groups are in contention; their leverage is greater and is usually applied with more sophistication; the stakes for which they compete are much higher. But the differences are matters of degree; the power structure of the U.S. as a whole is analogous to the system at state and local levels. The nation has, for instance, a power elite that in principle is not all that different from a small town's leading citizens gathering at the coffee shop.

A 1970 study of public and private positions of national authority revealed some surprising statistics. Barely 4,000 people in about 5,400 key decision-making positions (some individuals filled more than one role) collectively controlled half the country's industrial assets, half its banking wealth, about half the wealth of private universities and foundations, and half of the nation's transportation, communications and utilities. This handful of people (less than two thousandths of one percent of the population) also ran the big television networks, newspaper chains and news wire services, the most important Washington and New York law firms, and the country's major cultural and civic organizations. And they held all the top jobs in the federal government — military as well as civilian.

While this seems to be an incredible concentration of power, pluralists argue that these people failed to constitute a true elite, in the sense that they were not closely associated in a tight clique of common background and common aims. The American system certainly does allow for more vertical mobility than most other societies, and some of the top people — especially those in military roles — rose from simple origins. Nonetheless, according to the criteria employed by Thomas R. Dye, the sociologist who made the study, fully 90 percent of the 4,000 were born into America's social and economic upper and upper-middle classes — classes that accounted for only 22 percent of the nation's population.

Moreover, quite a few of the 4,000 were personally acquainted with one another. They had met either through their work, through ultraselective social organizations such as California's Bohemian Club *(page 120)* or through such extremely influential policy-planning groups as the Council on For-

Citizens of Burke Hollow, Vermont, pledge allegiance to the flag at the opening of the annual town meeting. Here, as in other small New England towns, voters speak out on local government, decide on tax rates and elect new town officials.

AN ENDURING PLAN OF GOVERNMENT

"The Constitution of the United States was made not merely for the generation that then existed," said 19th-century American statesman Henry Clay, "but for posterity — unlimited, undefined, endless, perpetual posterity." The genius of the Founding Fathers was to set out a plan incorporating an array of checks and balances. Powers were distributed among three branches of government — the executive, legislative and judicial.

The president, as chief executive, is the single most powerful individual in government. He can veto legislation passed by the Congress and initiate legislation of his own. He is commander-in-chief of the armed forces and head of his political party. The president appoints his cabinet but he must get the Senate's approval of his appointments. He also appoints the heads of the numerous governmental agencies.

The two houses of Congress, the Senate and the House of Representatives, restrain the president's power. They initiate legislation of their own, act on or vote down presidential proposals, and can overturn a presidential veto on a bill if two thirds of the members of both houses agree. Senators are elected every six years, two from each state, while representatives are voted in for two-year terms from 435 congressional districts. By establishing two houses in Congress, the framers of the Constitution guaranteed that no single group would make the laws.

The Supreme Court can declare invalid any legislation or congressional or presidential decisions deemed incompatible with the Constitution. The nine justices of the court are appointed by the president — with the Senate's approval — and have life tenure.

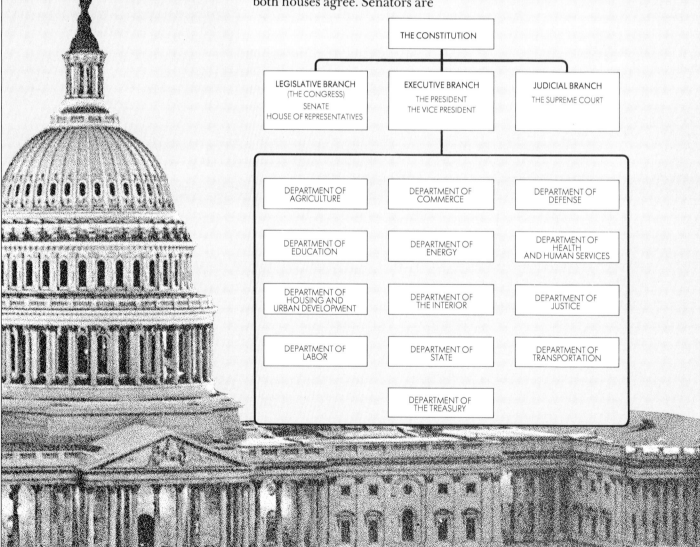

THE CONSTITUTION

LEGISLATIVE BRANCH
(THE CONGRESS)
SENATE
HOUSE OF REPRESENTATIVES

EXECUTIVE BRANCH
THE PRESIDENT
THE VICE PRESIDENT

JUDICIAL BRANCH
THE SUPREME COURT

DEPARTMENT OF AGRICULTURE

DEPARTMENT OF COMMERCE

DEPARTMENT OF DEFENSE

DEPARTMENT OF EDUCATION

DEPARTMENT OF ENERGY

DEPARTMENT OF HEALTH AND HUMAN SERVICES

DEPARTMENT OF HOUSING AND URBAN DEVELOPMENT

DEPARTMENT OF THE INTERIOR

DEPARTMENT OF JUSTICE

DEPARTMENT OF LABOR

DEPARTMENT OF STATE

DEPARTMENT OF TRANSPORTATION

DEPARTMENT OF THE TREASURY

eign Relations, the Business Council and the Committee for Economic Development, which devote private money and effort to finding solutions to public problems.

Eminence has its own rewards, and those who have made it to the top find it easy to circulate in the company of other movers and shakers. The interrelationships of America's powerful can be glimpsed by taking note of just a few of the men who were members of both the Council on Foreign Relations and New York's Century Club during the late 1960s. Among a bevy of corporate chiefs, leading bankers and top-flight lawyers were editors of *Time, Newsweek* and *The New York Times,* multimillionaires John D. Rockefeller III and his brothers Nelson and David, perennial presidential advisor Henry Kissinger, prominent newspaper columnists Walter Lippmann and James Reston, then-Secretary of State Dean Rusk, a deputy secretary of defense, the president of the CBS broadcasting network and the chairman of the Ford Foundation.

Viewed from another perspective, however, the elite can appear much less formidable. In the first place, power in the U.S. is probably more widely dispersed than in many other major nations. It is likely, for instance, that the equivalent of the power exercised by those 4,000 Americans is concentrated in the hands of a few dozen individuals in a country like the Soviet Union.

Furthermore, the composition of the U.S. elite is constantly shifting as the mighty rise and fall, retire or die, and — especially — as voters oust one of the two major political parties from governmental office and replace it with the other.

In fact, the elite discerned by sociologist Dye in his 1970 study would have had a different complexion if examined again little more than a decade later. In 1970 a loose-knit coalition of Democratic and Republican politicians, bankers, lawyers, industrialists and media people — tagged "the Eastern liberal establishment" because of its members' political philosophies and the fact that most operated from power bases in the northeastern United States — was a loud and influential voice in American political life. But in subsequent years it lost much influence to challengers that Dye labeled the "Sun Belt cowboys," political conservatives from the West and South, newly rich in oil, aerospace and real estate-boom money, and riding a tide of public resentment of high taxes and pervasive bureaucracy.

Another factor that restricts the power of any American national elite — and the power of the two major political parties themselves — is the complex and unwieldy lawmaking process. Under the parliamentary system used by most European nations, the party with a majority of legislators forms a government that can, generally speaking, put its programs into effect with little difficulty. But under the American system, the party of the president might control only one — or perhaps neither — of the two lawmaking bodies of Congress, the Senate and the House of Representatives. In any case, both the Republican and Democratic parties encompass such wide ideological spectrums that neither one can depend on all of its senators and representatives to agree on any given proposal.

Thus, as a bill (a proposed new law) makes its way through the labyrinth of committees and subcommittees in both houses, the contending legislators each give a little and get a little, lubricating the process with compromise. "The oil-can is mightier than the sword," said the late Senator Everett Dirksen, a master at the game.

At every turn, legislators are subject to blandishments and pressures from outside forces — sometimes a lawmaker's home-state constituents, but more often some of the 6,000 lobbyists who work for special-interest groups such as corporations, veterans or farmers. Lobbyists do not always get what they want, but they are usually given a hearing because they take pains to cultivate legislators, doing favors for them and often helping finance their election campaigns. Of the 25,000 or so bills introduced in Congress over a two-year period, as few as 700 may become law.

To steer a bill through this political obstacle course, a politician must employ clever strategies and win influential support at key points of decision. "Once begin the dance of legislation," said President Woodrow Wilson, "and you must struggle through its mazes as best you can to the breathless end — if any end there be." An example of what Wilson meant — and a revealing lesson in the realities of the American power structure — is the odyssey undertaken by first-term Senator Pete V. Domenici, a Republican from New Mexico, when he set out in February 1977 to secure a relatively minor piece of legislation: a law that would require users of inland waterways to help the federal government pay for the waterways' construction and maintenance.

Whereas trucking lines paid tolls, license fees and fuel taxes to help subsidize highways — and railroads built and maintained their own tracks — water-cargo carriers, which hauled 16 percent of the nation's inland freight, contributed not a penny toward the cost of dams, locks, dredging and upkeep of

5

the 25,000-mile waterway system. All of the work was done at public expense by the U.S. Army Corps of Engineers.

Domenici, who served on the Senate's Environment and Public Works Committee, considered the free use of waterways to be clearly inequitable — perhaps particularly so because he came from a state that had no barge lines and lots of railroads. His interest in the question became charged with fervor one day during a hearing on the need to rebuild a large waterway facility in Illinois called Lock and Dam 26. He casually asked witnesses, who included representatives of inland shipping companies, whether the barge industry itself should not pay for the new construction. "Some of those barge guys jumped right out of their skins when I brought it up," he later recalled. Indeed, one of them shouted angrily, "You don't have any waterways in New Mexico. What business is it of yours?"

"Mister," replied Domenici, his temper igniting, "you're going to find out what business it is of mine." He then turned to two aides and snapped, "Get me a user-charge bill."

The aides drafted legislation that set up a system of waterway user fees. But similar bills had been proposed many times in the past, and all had collapsed under pressure from barge interests and their powerful advocates in Congress, who liked the cheap shipping rates that farmers and manufacturers in their home states enjoyed from the barge lines. Rather than confront the opposition head on, Domenici tried a congressional tactic known as piggybacking. He attached his proposal to a piece of legislation that barge owners eagerly supported: a bill to spend $400 million to rebuild Lock and Dam 26.

Railroad lobbyists, of course, were

PLAYGROUND OF THE POWERFUL

What has been called "the greatest men's party on earth" takes place every July at a California campsite called Bohemian Grove, located in a 2,700-acre redwood forest 65 miles north of San Francisco. The party consists of a huge two-week camp-out attended by more than 2,000 men (and men only).

It is a remarkable gathering largely because these 2,000 include many of the richest and most powerful individuals in America, from the presidents of the nation's largest corporations and banks to presidents of the United States.

The Grove and its camp buildings are owned by San Francisco's Bohemian Club, founded in 1872 as a refuge for writers, actors and other "bohemians" of the arts. The club was soon taken over, however, by the city's merchants and moneymen, and it has been a bastion of the well-to-do ever since.

The July camp sessions, begun in 1878, were once simply informal get-togethers *(below)*, but soon became known (though not widely known) as meetings of the mighty.

Today, a majority of the club's members remain Californians, but men from most of the other 49 states also hold coveted memberships. Presidents Herbert Hoover, Richard Nixon and Ronald Reagan have belonged to the club, as have many secretaries of state, commerce and defense. Although the ostensible purpose is relaxation, two weeks of proximity helps knit together these members of the power elite. The Grove has long been, as one journalist put it, "a major showcase," where the leaders in business and politics, in education and the arts "can come to examine each other" — and to make many momentous decisions about the nation's future.

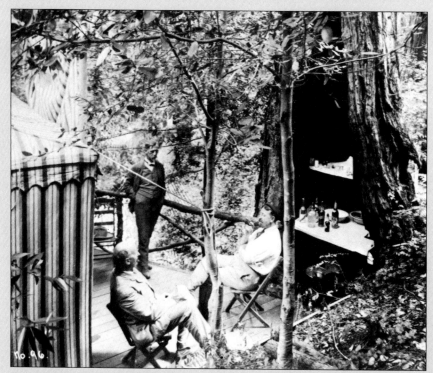

Club members relax at Bohemian Grove in 1907, 29 years after the first outing.

delighted with Domenici's proposal. So were environmentalists, who had long been unhappy that barge traffic and excessive construction of dams and locks destroyed wildlife habitats, reduced the recreational use of rivers and polluted public waters. But that support was more than offset by Domenici's potential antagonists, among them such powerful river-state senators as Louisiana's Russell B. Long, chairman of the Finance Committee, Mississippi's John C. Stennis, head of the Armed Forces Committee, and the state of Washington's Warren G. Magnuson, steward of the Commerce Committee.

Domenici knew his bill would never reach the Senate floor for a vote if he launched it solely in one of the committees ruled by these user-fee opponents. But since it would be impolitic to try to hurdle all of them at the outset, Domenici had the bill sent, simultaneously, to the Commerce Committee and to his own Public Works Committee. A favorable recommendation from only one committee would bring the bill to the Senate floor for debate.

The Republican senator got some help from Democratic President Jimmy Carter's administration when Transportation Secretary Brock Adams testified at a hearing on the proposal. "It is simply not just," Adams declared, "that profit-making businesses should have this much of their costs met by the American taxpayer." Domenici also got an unexpected boost from Illinois's Republican Senator Charles H. Percy, who risked antagonizing his own constituents by declaring, "I am absolutely convinced, and have told the barge owners this, the free ride is over. To keep up these waterways, the user must pay for the service." Buoyed by this support, Domenici steered the com-

bined Lock 26 and user-fee bill to a 14-to-1 endorsement by the full committee. This was in May of 1977.

With the bill headed for a debate on the Senate floor, Domenici managed to enlist more help from President Carter, who made it known that he would "veto any bill authorizing construction of a new Lock and Dam 26 which does not also contain a provision for waterway user charges."

A preliminary nose count in the Senate indicated that the vote would be close, with about 40 senators lined up on each side and 20 uncommitted. It was now June, and lobbyists went to work on the uncommitted. J. D. Feeney, the genial ("Call me Joe") general counsel of the Western Railroads Association, captained the lobbying team on Domenici's side, while cocky St. Louis lawyer Louis B. Susman, a well-connected member of the Democratic National Committee, became the chief persuader for the barge owners. Each side had put together a war chest of about $500,000, mainly from corporate contributions.

While the barge interests had financed their lobbyists openly, the pro-Domenici forces had been faced by a special problem that required a delicate solution. Although they could count on the railroads for support, they could ill afford to have them as allies: The railroads were the barge industry's competition, and their motives were bound to be regarded as suspect. So the pro-Domenici forces tried another tack. They turned to the environmentalists, who they knew were opposed to the barge interests, and arranged for the railroads to give them financial aid. The environmentalists, however, had reservations. "If you ever wanted to see a bunch of people who were skittish

about dealing with railroads," chortled Joe Feeney, "it was those bearded environmentalists. Hell, some of those guys had sued us a few times."

Feeney arranged a bit of dubious but time-honored Washington hanky-panky: He set up what is called a laundry, a bank account in the name of a bogus organization. The name of the organization was the Council for a Sound Waterway Policy, and the address on its letterhead was a vacant railroad office. Through it, Feeney pumped up to $5,000 a month to environmental groups, thus enabling them to lobby effectively on behalf of the bill.

Probably the most bizarre aspect of the lobbying campaign's finances was the role of United States Steel; it actually managed to lobby on both sides of the question. United States Steel's wholly owned subsidiary, the Elgin, Joliet and Eastern Railroad, gave several thousand dollars to support the user-fee proposal, while another United States Steel satrapy, the Ohio Barge Line, Inc., donated similar funds to try to defeat the measure.

The final days before the June vote provided a textbook display of behind-the-scenes activity in Congress. Domenici tried to nail down the votes of three Western Republicans for his bill, but he learned that Senator Stennis had captured their allegiance by threatening to oppose funding for an irrigation project they wanted for their states. President Carter won the support of West Virginia's Senator Jennings Randolph by promising to campaign for him. And Russell Long guaranteed favorable Finance Committee action on a tax bill backed by a Delaware Republican in return for that senator's vote against the user fee.

When Long learned that two pro-

5

user-fee senators had gone out of town on other business, he tried a tough-minded ploy, calling for an immediate vote on June 22. To the astonishment of Senate veterans, Domenici's bill was passed, 71 votes to 20. "You'll never guess what happened," a reporter was heard yelling into a telephone. "Pete Domenici went head to head with Russell Long, and Domenici won!"

The victory was short-lived. The bill contained a serious flaw: According to the Constitution, all revenue-raising laws must originate in the House of Representatives. Domenici had hoped his proposal would be interpreted as a regulatory measure, rather than a revenue bill. But the chairman of the House Ways and Means Committee, Oregon's Al Ullman, was having none of that. He tersely informed the Senate that it had violated the Constitution. The Domenici bill was stuck.

At this critical point, the Democratic administration gave more help to the Republican senator. It enlisted the aid of Thomas P. "Tip" O'Neill Jr., who — as leader of the Democratic majority in the lower legislative body — was Speaker of the House. A master with the oil-can, the crafty, imposing, white-haired Boston Irishman convinced leading members of Congress that the Domenici bill ought to be introduced as a brand-new measure in the House. But the representatives added a provision that dismayed Domenici: Instead of a direct user fee, revenues would come from a tax on barge diesel fuel. And the tax would be only four to six cents per gallon, low enough for barge owners to accept. On October 13, the House passed the measure, 331 to 70.

The bill then moved back to the Senate, where Domenici sought a way to restore his principle of payments di-

rectly related to use. Meanwhile, the bargemen, who had been amenable to compromise in the House, began to talk tough again. They wanted the bill stopped. That was too much for Russell Long, whose credo as a senator was negotiation and accommodation. "I'm likely to get a little perturbed with these fellows," he remarked. "There comes a time when you have to get realistic and give an inch or two. That's how legislating works."

Long and Domenici, both fearing they might lose a straight vote on the Senate floor, tried through intermediaries to reach a compromise. But the effort was unsuccessful. "They're like a pair of sumo wrestlers," said one observer. "They dance around throwing salt in the air, but they're afraid to get in the ring." Domenici finally struck a bargain with another opponent of his proposal, Illinois Democrat Adlai E. Stevenson. The two men crafted a measure that included both the diesel tax and a separate, modest-sized user fee. President Carter announced that the Stevenson-Domenici compromise was the minimum he would accept.

But when the revised bill reached the Senate floor in May 1978, the farm lobby, concerned that the user fee would increase farmers' freight rates, joined the barge interests in opposing it, and some farm-state senators who had been supporters became foes. Several other senators, because they were up for reelection in 1978, could no longer afford to oppose the rivermen in their home states. This time the Senate voted Domenici's bill down, 47 to 43, accepting instead the diesel-tax measure passed by the House. On hearing the news, President Carter promised to veto the bill if it reached his desk.

Now nobody had anything to show

for all the months of hard, abrasive work. The barge industry was getting no new Lock and Dam 26; Domenici's user-fee principle was out the window; the president appeared in an unpopular negative position; and the river-state legislators had gained nothing for the folks back home. Suddenly both camps seemed ready for serious and sustained negotiations.

Together they came up with a well-oiled compromise: A new Inland Waterways Trust Fund would be created by the bill. The trust would receive the diesel-tax monies (with the tax rate now raised to 10 cents a gallon), and the revenue would be entirely devoted to maintaining the waterways. And, of course, the package featured a rebuilt Lock and Dam 26.

Long, Domenici and Carter all endorsed the amended measure. By the time the much-repaired bill was ready for a vote on October 6, however, only eight days remained in the 1978 congressional session, and there was no telling how the measure might fare if it was held over till the next Congress. Urgent action by a master of parliamentary tactics was required. Russell Long agreed to provide it. "We just have to find a vehicle, and that's no problem," he said. "I've always got a few little bills back in the office."

What Long meant was that he would attach the waterways measure to some minor bill that had already passed the House and was resting in his Senate office, awaiting a propitious moment. When the "little bill" went to the Senate floor, the real issue could be attached to it as an amendment. Senator Long rooted out a measure that authorized certain charitable organizations to run tax-free bingo games. The odd combination of a bingo measure and

A HOUSE FOR ALL THE PEOPLE

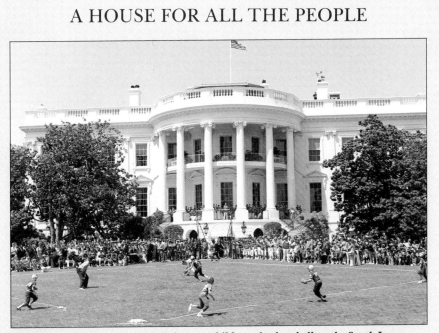

During a celebration of the national game, children play baseball on the South Lawn.

Thomas Jefferson, the first president to spend a full term living in the White House, helped set the tone for that handsome mansion, as he did for many American institutions. Arranging a dinner during his 1801-1809 tenure in office, he invited several important officials — and then added his butcher's name to the guest list.

History fails to record whether any subsequent presidents have invited their suppliers of chops and roasts to dine. But the executive mansion has remained what President Franklin D. Roosevelt called it, "a house owned by all the American people." A number of the rooms are open to the public five days each week; in recent years about 1.5 million visitors have toured the mansion annually, or have attended such yearly events as the egg-rolling for children at Easter and the spring garden tour. And there are many other informal events, even including games on the lawn (above). It seems safe to say that in no other nation is the chief executive's residence so available to the citizenry.

Not all of the White House's 132 rooms are, of course, open to the public. Twenty-five rooms on the second and third floors provide private living quarters for the presidential family. These include a small kitchen and dining room. For formal entertaining of foreign heads of state and other dignitaries there are two principal rooms, the State Dining Room and the East Room.

This large establishment requires more than 85 full-time employees, from cooks to electricians to a cleaning staff (which uses 3,000 pounds of detergent each year), plus 17 gardeners to care for the 18 acres of grounds. The kitchen where large banquets are prepared has four full-time chefs. The budget for official entertaining, voted by Congress, exceeds $200,000 a year. The number of guests attending White House functions can top 75,000 annually.

But even the most august affairs are relatively modest. The State Dining Room seats a maximum of 140. Even the name of the building reflects a certain modesty. It is the "White House" for a quite mundane reason. British troops set fire to the building during the War of 1812; it has been painted white ever since to hide the ugly burn marks on the stone walls.

the waterways legislation quickly came to the floor, and the Senate passed it by a unanimous voice vote.

Now the jerry-built measure had to get through the House of Representatives, since it was no longer the mere bingo bill previously passed by that body. O'Neill, who had been brought into Long's plan, was ready. Under a special provision known as suspension, he brought the bill directly onto the floor for a fast vote — with no stops in committees along the way. When the tally was taken — a year and seven months after the New Mexico senator had introduced his original bill and only 26 hours before Congress was scheduled to adjourn — Pete Domenici had won at last, 287 to 123.

Thus are most laws in Washington created, by canny legislators who can get the business accomplished. But occasionally the system must respond to an anguished cry for justice or progress from the nation as a whole, or from a large section of the population. At such times the needed legislation may be fashioned and driven into being by political adroitness outside the formal lawmaking process as well as inside it. That was the case in the 1960s, when a black preacher named Martin Luther King Jr. led a drive to secure full voting rights for America's blacks.

In many parts of the South, literacy tests, poll taxes and physical intimidation had been used to keep blacks away from the ballot boxes and politically powerless. For example, the literacy test for voter registration in Alabama's Dallas County — given only twice a month — required that an applicant write from dictation a part of the Constitution and answer eight questions on the governmental process. Although the county's population was almost 60 percent black, 9,542 local whites made it onto the voting rolls while only 335 blacks qualified.

At that pace, protested King, who had been organizing demonstrations for racial equality since the 1950s, "it would take 103 years to register the adult Negroes." And those blacks who tried to assert their right to vote were likely to be manhandled by Dallas County Sheriff Jim Clark, whose deputies used electric cattle prods to deter demonstrators.

King chose the town of Selma, the Dallas County seat, as the crucible for forging a new law to end voter discrimination once and for all. His strategy was to dramatize the plight of Southern blacks through confrontations between peaceable marchers and hot-tempered, armed local police. King believed that national press coverage of attacks on his people would arouse the conscience of the nation.

In January 1965, he led 400 blacks in the first of several marches to the Dallas County courthouse in Selma. Events developed as King had foreseen. A photograph showing Sheriff Clark roughing up a woman protestor appeared in Northern newspapers. A few days later, Clark clubbed another woman while two other officers held her down. King was jailed for violating a town ordinance against unauthorized parades, and 500 protesting schoolchildren also were locked up. New York Senator Jacob K. Javits called the arrests "shocking," and a group of liberal congressmembers made plans to visit Selma. "There are more Negroes in jail with me," King wrote, "than there are on the voting rolls."

President Lyndon B. Johnson made it known he was ready for quick and serious talks with King about legislation to end voting discrimination. The black leader posted bail, and a couple of days later he flew to Washington to meet with President Johnson. King said he favored a voting-rights bill that would cover both state and federal elections, eliminate literacy tests and empower federal officials to enforce fair registration procedures. Johnson's aides began drawing up just such a bill, and King returned to the South to keep the pres-

Linking arms with other civil-rights leaders, the Reverend Martin Luther King Jr. *(second from right)* marches in Memphis, Tennessee, to demonstrate for equal rights, a week before his assassination in April 1968.

sure up, telling his followers, "We are going to bring a voting bill into being in the streets of Selma."

The struggle was getting bloody. On February 18, an Alabama state trooper shot and mortally wounded 26-year-old protestor Jimmy Lee Jackson while he walked with other blacks in a demonstration in the adjacent county. On March 7, King's deputy Hosea Williams was leading some 525 protestors across a Selma bridge on the start of a 54-mile hike to the state capital of Montgomery when about 50 state policemen and several dozen local officers, some on horseback, charged into the crowd in a flying wedge, tossing tear gas and flailing the blacks with clubs and whips. "The wedge moved with such force that it seemed almost to pass over the waiting column instead of through it," a journalist reported.

Several protestors lay wounded while lawmen chased other demonstrators through the streets of Selma. Many blacks suffered broken ribs, head gashes and other injuries. That evening, viewers all across the nation saw the brutal assault on television newscasts. Two days later, racist thugs beat up and mortally injured a white minister named James Reeb, who had traveled south from Boston to offer his moral support to the protest.

Hundreds of outraged people from all over the U.S. — students, clergymen, housewives — flocked to Selma to enlist in King's army. While pickets demanding action staged a sit-in at the White House in Washington, administration attorneys hurried to finish a draft bill. At the end of the week President Johnson told a joint session of Congress that the legislation was ready. "Their cause must be our cause too," he said of King's legions. "It is all of us who must

overcome the crippling legacy of bigotry and injustice."

More and more aroused Americans journeyed to Alabama to join the movement. Alabama Governor George C. Wallace, who had tried to prohibit the demonstrations, telegraphed the president that the state lacked the means to protect either marchers or sympathetic bystanders. That was too much for Lyndon Johnson. He federalized the Alabama National Guard, putting that state militia's officers under his direct orders to prevent further violence.

Meanwhile, the voting-rights bill had acquired irresistible support. The president, leaders of both parties, the national press, churches and labor unions had all joined the black civil rights leaders in advocating prompt enactment. The bill that arrived in the Senate from the president instantly acquired sponsorship by a bipartisan coalition of 66 senators.

During the debate a few Southern senators challenged the measure, arguing that states had the right to set their own voting standards. But after offering a desultory flurry of amendments, opponents of the bill fell back, demoralized. "I assume the die is cast," sighed Georgia's Senator Richard Russell.

In Alabama, meanwhile, some 25,000 people, white and black, had descended on Montgomery, where they were protected by the National Guard. "We are on the move now," King told them. "We are moving to the land of freedom." That same night a white woman from Detroit, Viola Liuzzo, was murdered in a Ku Klux Klan ambush as she rode in a car traveling toward Montgomery. She was the last casualty in the crusade for a law to guarantee equality at the polls.

The following week, the U.S. Senate

passed the Voting Rights Act of 1965 by a stunning majority of 77 to 19. The bill then stalled in the House for several weeks, because of the recalcitrance of Rules Committee Chairman Howard Smith of Virginia. He called the measure unconstitutional, asserting that it was "dripping in venom" and that it would allow the U.S. Attorney General "almost unlimited power to investigate, to prosecute and to try and convict sovereign states."

But many of his own Southern colleagues thought otherwise. Louisiana's Hale Boggs said in a speech to the House, "I love my state. I love the South. I support this bill because I believe the fundamental right to vote must be a part of this great experiment in human progress under freedom which is America." The House finally passed the bill by a vote of 333 to 85.

When President Johnson signed the act into law on August 6, he declared that "the last of the legal barriers" to racial equality had come down. Before the end of the month, 27,385 blacks had been registered as voters by federal examiners in Alabama, Louisiana and Mississippi.

In the ensuing decade and beyond, the law was to alter the contours of Southern politics, as blacks in large numbers exercised their franchise for the first time. President Johnson called the Voting Rights Act "one of the most monumental laws in the history of American freedom." He could rightly have added that the story of the law's creation was itself a monument — a monument to a system that is often clumsy, that sometimes evokes justifiable cynicism by favoring the powerful, but that has proved its ability, when pressed, to serve democratically the needs of all the people. □

REDEFINING WOMEN'S ROLES

The smiling police officer at right represents a dramatic change in American life: recruit Beth Atkins of the Chicago Police Department is one of the more than 45 million women in the United States now working. In the early 1960s, only 40 percent of the female population between the ages of 20 and 34 held jobs outside the home. Today, the proportion is two thirds, and it is estimated that 95 percent of American women aged 25 to 34 will be working by 1995. Moreover, women are turning away from the "pink collar" clerical and secretarial jobs they have traditionally held in great numbers and are joining the ranks of doctors, lawyers, airline pilots and other professions once almost exclusively held by men.

What this social revolution means in domestic terms can be seen in the daily routine of Chicago police officers Beth and Mike Atkins and their daughters, Amy, 11, and Eileen, nine. The Atkinses are fortunate because Mike, who has been a detective on the police force for more than a decade, can select his work shift so as to be home while Beth is on patrol. Amy and Eileen have become more independent and like having time with each parent. Combined paychecks give the family money to spend on weekly family outings.

The Atkinses have discovered that they all must be more considerate of one another. Once, after tidying up the house and going to work, Beth returned to find objects and clothes scattered about. There was a polite but strained family conference, and since then Mike and the girls have taken responsibility for cleaning up whatever mess they create. Mike, in agreeing to share some of the household chores, has begun to do the ironing.

Amused by an exchange heard on her radio, Chicago police officer Beth Atkins shares the remark with her training officer, Jack Murphy. As a recruit, she will patrol with a training officer for three months.

Beth runs her daily six miles through the neighborhood, accompanied by Amy on her bicycle. Although her most arduous previous exercise was shopping, Beth is now so fit that she has been named top female athlete in her class of recruits.

Rushing off to work at 7:20 a.m., Beth gives her husband a quick kiss. She has made breakfast for him and daughters Eileen *(left)* and Amy. Mike will drive the girls to school.

Lined up at the lockers with fellow recruits, Beth joins the discussion after a police academy class on defense tactics.

On patrol in Chicago's North Side, Jack Murphy and Beth Atkins write up a disturbance-of-the-peace report *(above, left)*. Later, Beth helps a victim of attempted robbery *(above, right)*, and keeps her sense of humor when a street vendor *(right)* responds to her request to move on with a cajoling, "You sure are pretty."

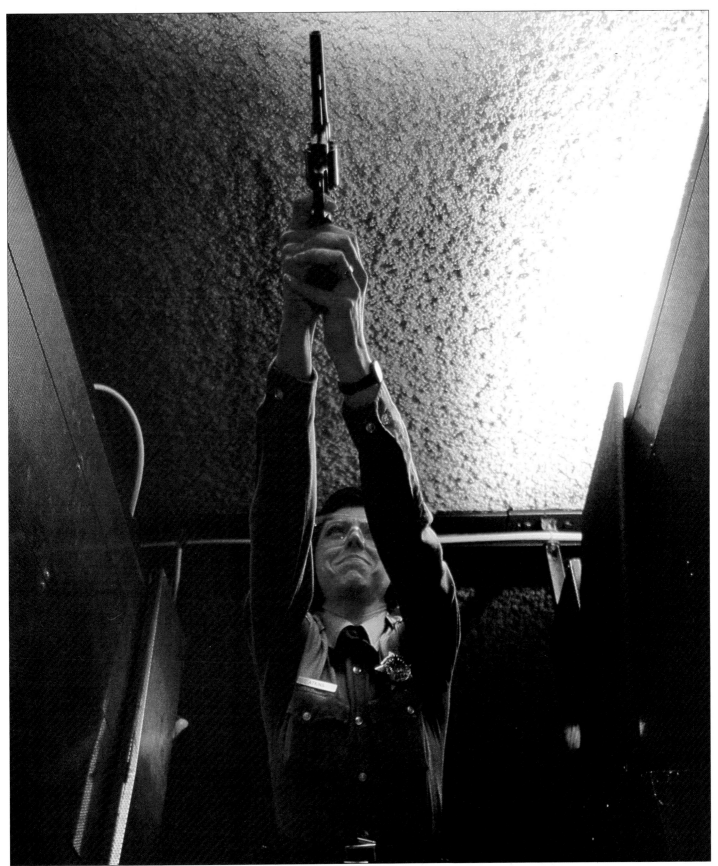

Beth practices regularly in the academy firing range. A crack shot, she ranked in the top 10 percent of her class.

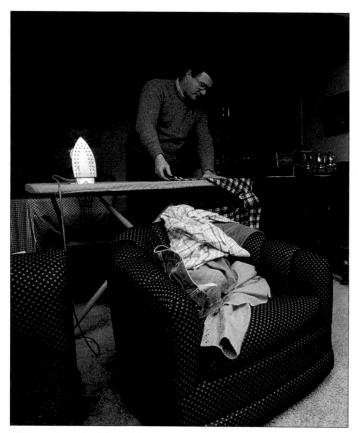

Mike watches television while
ironing, a chore that convention would
prevent men in many other
countries from taking on.

Making the most of their time with
their daughters, Mike and Beth say an
affectionate good-night to Eileen
(left) and Amy. As part of a regular
ritual, all four pray together before
the lights are turned off.

Pillared porticos, lush lawns and
backyard swimming pools proclaim
the prosperity of those who have
made it in the coal-mining town of
Pikeville, Kentucky. "We're not the
idle rich," says one resident of this
plush subdivision. "We're working
wealthy, not investor wealthy."

THE AMERICAN DREAM

A jetliner bearing the Great Seal of the United States touched down at West Berlin's Tempelhof Airport and rolled to a stop. Out onto the red-carpeted gangway stepped W. Michael Blumenthal, U.S. Secretary of the Treasury, on a government mission. A cluster of dignitaries moved forward to greet him, and to walk him past a military honor guard to a waiting limousine.

Someone handed Blumenthal a local morning paper. There on the front page was his picture, along with a biographical sketch pointing out that the secretary, in making this brief visit to Berlin in February 1978, was in fact returning to his native city. It was true: A member of the U.S. Cabinet, and an American citizen for most of his adult life, Michael Blumenthal was by birth a Berliner, the son of a Jewish shopkeeper. "I thought it was coming full circle," he said, "that the people who had kicked me out now would put my picture on the front page and call me proudly a 'Berliner.'" And as he read through the story, his mind drifted back to the day, nearly 40 years earlier, when he and his family had fled Nazi Germany, and to the sequence of events that had carried him around the world to America — and to the highest levels of personal achievement. It was a classic tale of an immigrant who made good, and it represented in clearest outline what the world has come to think of as the American Dream.

The Blumenthals had left Germany in 1938, when Michael was 12. Their destination was Shanghai, then an open city where no special papers were required. There, Michael's parents scrounged a living, selling clothing while Michael attended a local British school. In 1942 the Japanese took over the city and herded them into a ghetto with the rest of Shanghai's refugees.

Release came in 1945, with the arrival of U.S. forces. The American soldiers, Blumenthal remembered, were "different from other people I knew — healthier, athletic, cleaner. They seemed more fun-loving, more joyful. And richer. Even the privates had what appeared to be a lot of money." But there was another difference that impressed him more. They were optimistic: "Most of them felt they had something going for them, and most felt that they could do what they wanted to do.

"I had lived in an environment, ever since I was old enough to realize what was going on, in which there were many, many restrictions placed on my ability to do the things I wanted to do," he recalled. Those restrictions "had nothing to do with me or with what I was capable of doing or willing to do. They had more to do with what my surname was, who my parents were, whether I had the right kind of passport, whether I was accepted in the right kind of school or the right kind of club, or whether I belonged to this group or that." The Americans he saw ignored such irrelevancies. "The aver-

6

age GI really exhibited the sense that, while he might be a corporal and someone else was a lieutenant or captain, he was as good as that person, even though one had a higher rank or was in a different category."

His reaction was clear. "I wanted to be like them. And I felt I could compete and do as well as they could."

Blumenthal eventually wangled a visa for the United States, stamped and signed on the back by the U.S. vice consul. He and his sister sailed for San Francisco in September 1947 aboard a converted troopship. Within five days of landing there, both had found jobs: she as a secretary, he as a billing clerk earning $40 a week.

It did not take Blumenthal long to discover that the fast track upward in America is through education. He enrolled in a junior college, took a second job running an elevator at St. Francis Hospital, and eventually transferred to the University of California at Berkeley, from which he graduated in 1951.

From then on, the path was clear. It carried the future Treasury Secretary to a doctorate from Princeton and the vice presidency of a small company. In 1960 there was a telephone call from the White House. "We're looking for people who have some business experience and some international economics background," said a presidential aide. "How would you like to work for the government?" Two months later he was in Washington as a deputy assistant secretary at the State Department.

On his first day in office, he hunted through the department telephone directory for the name of the vice consul who, 14 years earlier, had signed his visa. "He had been a demi-god to me," Blumenthal remembered, "but there was, of course, no reason why he should remember me. He had given visas to thousands of people." So the man was understandably mystified by a call from a high official.

"Yes, sir, what can I do for you?"

"Well, I'd like to have lunch with you," said Blumenthal.

"Do I know you?"

"I'll explain it all when I see you."

The two men met in the Secretaries' dining room, which was reserved for

A river of runners engulfs six lanes of highway just after the start of the annual New York City Marathon. So popular has the race become among physical-fitness buffs that the number of runners has to be limited by a lottery to 16,000 each year.

officials of senior rank and thus represented something of a treat for Blumenthal's guest. Blumenthal pulled out his old Shanghai identity card, frayed and rumpled with time, and handed it across the table. The man examined it, turned it over, and there on the back was the visa with his signature. "Well, I'll be damned," he said.

Since then Blumenthal has moved onward and upward, from government to private business and back again. But that stroke of recognition in the State Department dining room remains perhaps his proudest memory, the moment when he felt he had truly arrived.

This rags-to-riches scenario has been acted out so many times in so many different ways by so many people — from the first settlers to more recent arrivals like Blumenthal — that it has become the essence of the American Dream. Yet material success is only one of many American Dreams. They exist in hundreds of shapes and variations, and find their realization in unnumbered circumstances. All of them share a belief in unlimited opportunity: a firm conviction that with effort and a bit of luck, almost anyone can make their life what they want it to be. "If one advances confidently in the direction of his dreams," said Yankee philosopher Henry David Thoreau, "and endeavors to live the life which he has imagined, he will meet with a success unexpected in common hours."

Perhaps the highest of these dreams is good works. Americans are indoctrinated to help their fellows. If they are driven to acquire wealth, they are also driven to give it away once acquired. The Rockefellers and Fricks are famous philanthropists, but most humanitarianism is supported by people unknown outside their own communi-

ties; the average American gives away about 2 percent of earned income. Between individual gifts and the gifts of the nation's tens of thousands of philanthropic foundations, the annual total of donations in the U.S. amounts to about $40 billion.

Material things do not figure at all in the dreams of many Americans. They seek to fulfill inner goals. Some follow their own visions of God; a recent count found 336,281 religious groups in the U.S. Others pursue the will-o'-the-wisp of constant change; for these restless, never-satisfied individuals the dream is always something new, something different. Americans move an average of 13 times during their lifetime (by contrast, Britons change residence eight times, Japanese five). They switch jobs about 10 times. In her book *Pathfinders*, journalist Gail Sheehy writes of a man who was, successively and generally successfully, a steelworker, soldier, financial researcher, investment adviser, stockbroker, ski instructor, teacher of the blind and town mayor.

The lure of easy change can lead many to turn away from the mainstream of society, giving up big-city life for some simple rural existence, or — more dramatically — becoming hedonistic wanderers living hand to mouth in a land of plenty. Some seek to create a better social system by establishing utopian communities. America has always been a haven for utopias; the first, Plockhoy's Commonwealth, was founded by Dutch Mennonite Pieter Plockhoy in 1663 along the Delaware River, and new ones continue to spring up.

All these dreams, some more admirable than others, depend on opportunity that is equal for all — the chance to "do what they wanted to do," in Blumenthal's words. America is the land of op-

portunity, according to the cliché. But in recent times the reality of the cliché has been challenged. Blumenthal could be the exception, not the rule.

The doubts are justified. Not all the early settlers made it, and neither have all later arrivals or their descendants. Many returned to the Old World; others lie in unmarked graves in potter's fields. From 1908 to 1923, 50 immigrants returned to southern Italy, Russia and the Balkan countries out of every 100 who came to the U.S. from there. Poverty, ethnic bigotry, a home environment different from that of the dominant culture (middle-class, Anglo-Saxon) may limit the chance to try for the dream. More than 30 million Americans now live below the poverty level. For members of racial minorities, the situation is the bleakest: The poverty rate among whites is 11 percent, but for Hispanics it is 26.5 percent; for blacks, 34.2 percent.

The unemployment rate for minorities is also high: In 1985 fewer than two thirds of black men had jobs, compared with about 75 percent of whites. And a disproportionate number of black

Sporting shamrocks on their hats — and braces on their teeth — teen-age girls celebrate St. Patrick's Day in Chicago. Similar festivities are held in other cities as well, wherever Irish-Americans are numerous.

6

teenagers are out of work: In 1954 almost 55 percent of them were employed; by 1985, only 25 percent — one in four — were working.

And yet the American Dreams are alive and well. People do get an opportunity — many opportunities — to make their lives what they want them to be. The evidence is obvious for the dream of material success. Blumenthal, it turns out, is no exception:

• William Black started out with a shelled-nuts stand in the Times Square theater district of New York City. At the time of his death he owned a citywide chain of lunch counters pulling in more than $100 million a year.

• Mo Siegel, a laid-back 20-year-old hippie, began combing the hills around his Colorado home for the ingredients of herbal teas; in six years his blends brought him his first million dollars.

• Jennifer Steves, a Philadelphia social worker, began buying run-down Victorian town houses, sprucing them up, and using the refurbished dwellings as collateral to buy more houses. She soon owned 30 properties, and had a personal fortune of two million dollars.

• Steven Jobs and Stephen Wozniak, college dropouts barely out of their teens, built their first home computer in Jobs's parents' garage in Los Altos, California. Within five years annual sales of their Apple computers had soared to $600 million, and the two founders were each worth hundreds of millions of dollars.

Financial success stories are easy to find. By the 1980s some 600,000 Americans were millionaires, and the number goes up about 10 percent a year.

The dream achieved can be seen in the sprawl of highways and split-level suburbs, of beach resorts and vacation homes, of shopping malls and gourmet supermarkets, and in the statistics of national well-being. The standard of living in the United States was the highest among the industrial countries in the mid-1980s, as reported by the Organization for Economic Cooperation and Development. Of the 80 million households in the U.S., 64 percent owned their own living quarters, 51 percent had more than one vehicle, and 55 percent had at least two TV sets. Almost 10 percent of American workers ran their own businesses, and 54 percent of all wage earners in 1982 held white-collar jobs. A carpenter or mechanic was paid about $18,000 a year, more than triple the average for manufacturing jobs in Greece or Taiwan.

The vitality of the success dream is perhaps best seen in the experience of the recent wave of immigrants from Asia and the Pacific. A few have made millions; many have found the solid middle-class comfort they hoped for.

Among the fastest climbers have been the Koreans — nearly 500,000 — who arrived in the U.S. after 1968, when anti-Asian immigration quotas were eased. Their enterprise is visible in most major American cities. In New York City they number 100,000, and in only a dozen years they have come to dominate the $500-million retail produce business, which distributes two million tons of fruits and vegetables a year. They own three quarters of the 1,200 or so fruit and vegetable stores in the metropolitan area.

Young Jun Kwon is typical of the Koreans who have made it in this backbreaking and stressful work. In 1973, after a stint in the Korean Army, he pulled up stakes and moved to New York to join his sister and brother-in-law. He got work as a janitor in a wire and cable company, and soon advanced

A TOUGH, UPWARD CLIMB

Before the Pilgrims arrived on the rocky shore of Massachusetts in 1620, there already were Europeans living in what would eventually become the United States. These settlers were the Spaniards of Florida and the Southwest.

Today Hispanics, such as tractor operator Isauro Ríos *(right),* are the country's fastest-growing minority. By official count, they number 16.9 million. Their ranks are continually swelled by immigrants arriving legally, at the rate of 250,000 a year, from the Caribbean and from Central and South America. Most of these are Mexicans, Puerto Ricans and Cubans. Many more Hispanics are entering the country illegally. The Census Bureau estimates that 1.4 million of the Hispanics counted in the most recent census had entered the country without proper immigration papers. At any particular time, there may be 480,000 to 1.22 million Mexican "illegals" working in the U.S., their numbers rising and falling with the seasonal availability of jobs in agriculture.

If the Hispanic-American population continues to increase at its present rate, Hispanics will outnumber U.S. blacks within the next decade, to become the country's largest minority. Already 25 cities have Hispanic communities of 50,000 or more. Los Angeles County alone counts more than 2.5 million Hispanics among its 7.9 million inhabitants.

The Hispanic groups are as different from one another as are their countries of origin or the U.S. locales in which most of them settle — Cubans in Florida, Puerto Ricans in New York, Mexicans in the West and Southwest. What they have most in common is a proud determination to enter the American mainstream despite the

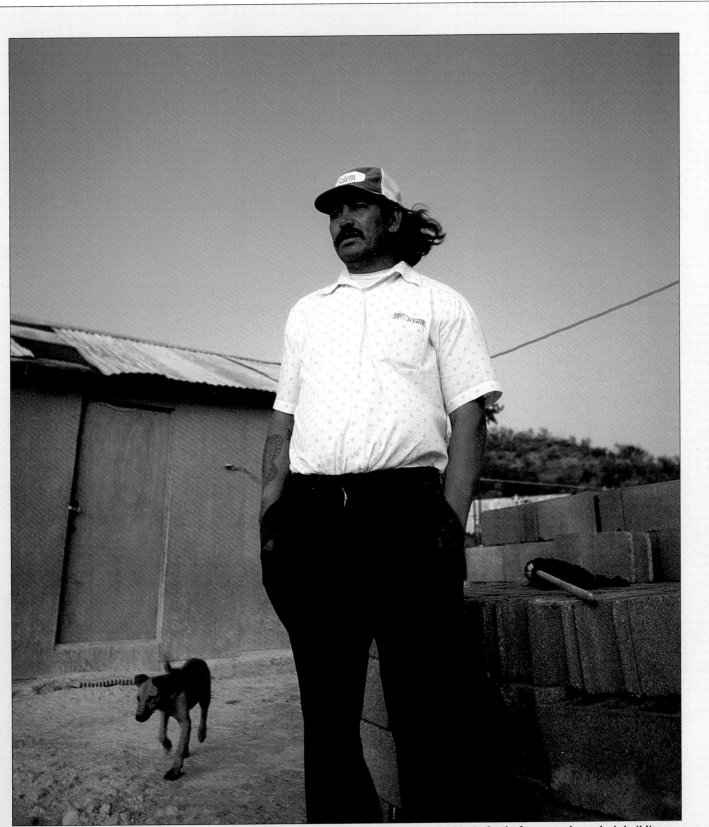

Tractor operator Isauro Ríos stands between his one-room plywood home and a pile of cinder blocks for the four-room house he is building.

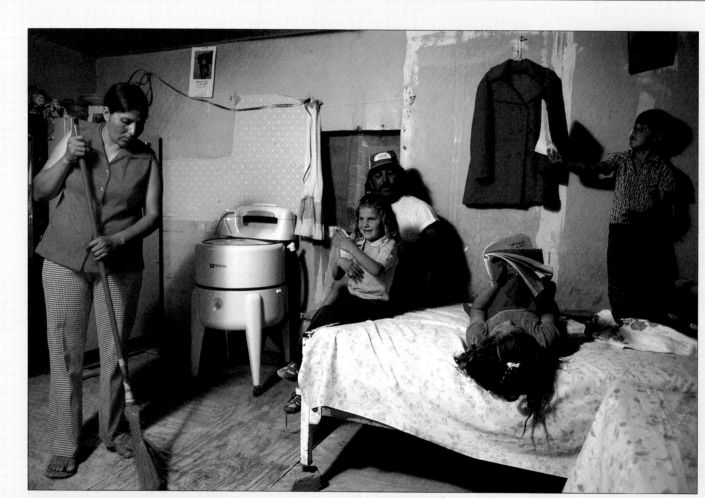

Wife María Jesús sweeps the floor of the Ríos house while Isauro relaxes with children María Oneida *(left)*, Wencelada and Juan Carlos.

political, economic and social barriers that most of them constantly encounter. And unlike many of the immigrants who preceded them, they wish to do so without having their own identities and culture subsumed as they become Americans. Some are insisting that Spanish, not English, be taught as a first language in the public schools their children attend.

Isauro Ríos is a stocky, horny-handed farm laborer living and working just across the Rio Grande from the land of his Mexican ancestors. He exemplifies many of the difficulties and, in even greater measure, the determination of his fellow Hispanics.

Isauro has some advantages over bewildered newcomers, and particularly over the apprehensive illegals, who throng the great metropolitan centers. American-born and bilingual, he was already in place, so to speak, before the great waves of Hispanic immigration began. But he happens to live and work in one of the Promised Land's least promising locations.

Home for Isauro is the tiny community of La Puerta in Starr County, down at the bottom of Texas and near the bottom of the U.S. economy. The county's population of 27,000 is 97 percent Hispanic, so that, unlike many other Spanish-Americans, Isauro does not lack political representation, at least at the local level, though this hardly translates into much in the way of economic benefits. Starr County residents had in the early 1980s a per capita annual income

A workday for Isauro begins at 6 a.m. as he prepares coffee and breakfast on the bottled-gas stove in the kitchen corner of the tiny house.

Isauro sees his children off to school. Sometimes he observes their classes.

of $2,668 and a median family income of $8,627. That makes Starr, according to the Census Bureau, one of the three poorest counties in a country with a then-national per capita income of $7,298 and a median family income of $19,917.

The Ríos family's income of $8,572 puts them below even the county's median, a fact that leaves Isauro undismayed. Mornings, he gets into his faded red 1976 Nova and heads for one of the county's big corporate-owned truck farms, where he drives a tractor 10 hours a day, seven days a week, at $3.45 an hour — 10 cents above the legal minimum wage. During a recent year, bad weather kept him idle about a third of the time, yet he considered himself lucky to have a steady job, in a county where un-

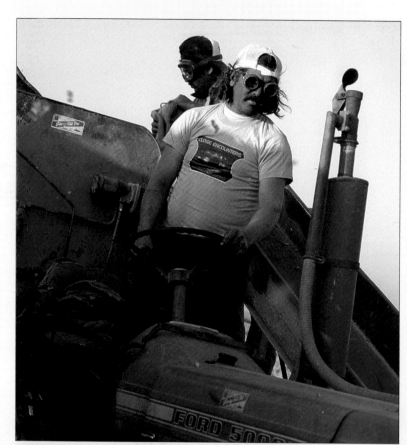

Begoggled against dust, Ríos delivers sacked onions to a pickup truck.

easy life. Born in La Puerta in 1948, he was one of 14 children (including one adoptee) of a Mexican-American father and a Mexican mother. Four of his siblings have died; the 10 survivors all still live and work in the area. Four graduated from high school, to the justified pride of their family (about half the students from Spanish-speaking homes in the U.S. become high-school dropouts). Isauro finished 10th grade and then went to work full time.

After a stint in the military, he returned to La Puerta. By 1977 he had acquired his present job and married a young Mexican woman six years his junior, whom he had first met at a dance in Starr County's one big town, Rio Grande City (population 8,930). On a plot of land bought from a neighbor, he and his wife, María Jesús, built a one-room home, 6 by 12 feet, floored with plywood and roofed with corrugated iron sheeting.

Four years later, Isauro and María Jesús began building a larger, cinder-block house on the slope behind their present one. With occasional help from a neighbor who

employment was more than three times the national average, and felt hopeful that he could eventually ascend to a less weather-sensitive job offering more hours of work and hence more money.

"There are people who work where I do that make $10,000 a year," he says. "Maybe soon I will make that much." Even if he does not, however, nothing will deter his drive toward a better life for himself and his family.

"Sometimes we are poor — when it rains, and I haven't been able to work," he says. "But I'm better off than most people. Sometimes when it rains, I go to school with my children. I see they have better shoes and better pencils than some of the other children. Then I think we're doing okay."

Though not stuck in one of the menial, dead-end jobs that are so often the lot of poor Hispanics, Isauro has had anything but an

Isauro checks a wall of the new home as María Jesús and two daughters look on.

144

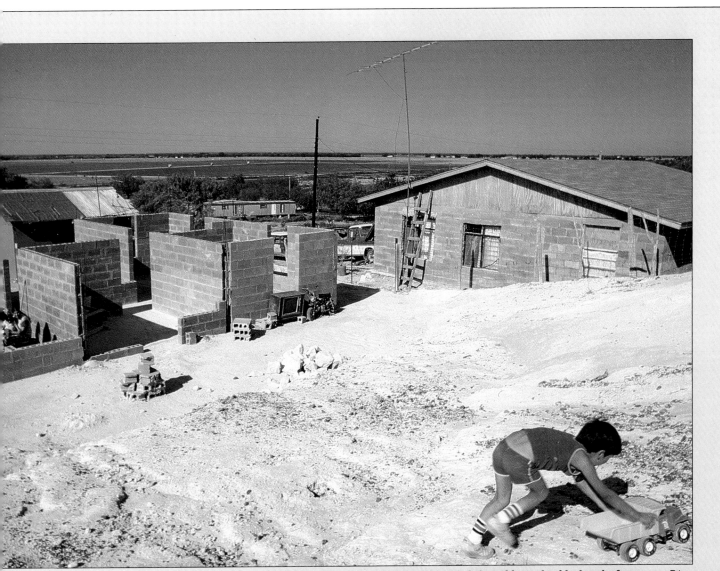

Juan Carlos concentrates on a project of his own while behind him his father adds another block to the future *casa Ríos*.

has completed a similar house, they have been working at it for two years, and since they have four growing children (Wencelada, 7; Juan Carlos, 6; María Oneida, 5; and baby Erica, 18 months), the need for more living space has become increasingly pressing.

With its three bedrooms, kitchen and indoor bathroom (replacing the present privy), the house will cost about $4,000. Work proceeds intermittently, whenever there is money for building materials to spare from his wages or what María Jesús earns from harvesting onions in the spring. "May-

be this year we'll finish it," says Isauro optimistically.

If not this year, then next, but finished it will be. Isauro Ríos is not easily diverted from his goals. He could earn more money as a migrant farm worker, as most of his neighbors do, but at the cost of dragging his family with him from job to job, depriving the children of schooling. "I want them to finish school," he says. "My son sometimes wants to go with me and ride on my tractor. But I always say I'm not taking him down there. I don't want him to learn to drive a tractor. I want him to go to college."

6

to foreman. Then he married, and his boss advised him: Start your own business. "All you'll ever get working for me is $400 or $500 a week," he was told.

So Kwon went into the grocery trade. Hours before dawn, Kwon is at the Hunts Point market — the city's main distribution center, in the South Bronx — selecting lettuce, onions, tomatoes, beans, oranges, apricots, persimmons and haggling over prices; then he loads the heavy crates into his truck. Back at his store, helped by his wife and brother, he scrubs each fruit and vegetable in cold water, polishes it dry, and stacks it into one of the tempting pyramids that have become a trademark of Korean grocers. At 8 a.m. he is open for business. For the next 12 hours the day stretches into a numbing routine of waiting on customers, restocking bins, tending the register. Then home to dinner, paperwork, a good-night kiss for his two small children and, finally, four or five hours of sleep before the next day starts.

Kwon's business is still small; he earns a bit more than he did as a foreman, but he never expects to get rich. "I am the first generation," he proclaims. "I am not working for myself. I am working for the second generation."

It is a time-honored sentiment in the United States. Nearly 200 years ago, John Adams, the nation's second president, wrote that he studied politics so that his sons might be free to engage in commerce and agriculture, and that their sons in turn might devote their energies to "painting, poetry, music, architecture." Indeed, he spawned an illustrious parade of statesmen, businessmen, historians, writers and art collectors. Kwon's children and grandchildren may well grow up to become doctors, or lawyers, or scientists, or

A child waits patiently while her mother examines the produce in a Chicago greengrocer's, one of hundreds of Korean-owned enterprises springing up around the country.

poets and artists. If so, they will have followed a well-trodden path to the realization of American Dreams.

That path is usually education. John Adams, son of a farmer, graduated from Harvard College in 1755. He applied his education to advance himself and to prepare the way for his descendants. People in the United States have been following his example ever since, aided by a system that is meant to be as egalitarian as possible. It differs from education in other countries in significant respects, providing never-ending opportunities to learn about an astonishing variety of subjects.

In most of the industrialized world, every child is expected to get about 10 years of basic schooling; but then, at the age of 18 or so, a strict selection process — the *baccalauréat* in France, the *Abitur* in West Germany, and the *Nyugaku shiken* in Japan — determines who goes on. Those who are not in the elite group chosen for further schooling are essentially barred from the higher levels of their societies. No such cutoff exists in the United States. Education may be no less crucial to success there than elsewhere, but it can be acquired at any age, in any of innumerable ways.

Horace Mann, the 19th-century edu-

cator considered the father of the American public-school system, called education "the great equalizer of the condition of men — the balance wheel of the social machinery." In the United States it has been just that. For the poor immigrants who poured into the country by the millions during the 19th century and the first part of the 20th, the basic public schools seemed heaven-sent. Here was a chance for their offspring to learn not only English, but American ways. By the early 20th century all American children were expected to complete 12 years of schooling; the high-school diploma thus earned became an essential passport to a good job. The number of years spent in school continued to increase, as first university training, then graduate study, became the norm.

Today, 86 percent of the population completes the 12 years of the public-school program, and 12.5 million are enrolled in colleges and universities. Most people pursuing higher education — proportionately more than in any other nation — do so in what has come to be considered the normal manner, that is, as full-time students in successive years of their youth. But this is not the only route to education.

As many as 42 percent of that 12.5 million attend class part time, many of them at night and many in community colleges like the one that helped Michael Blumenthal get started. Some four million study at home with printed correspondence courses. Opportunities for education are always available, everywhere and at every stage of life. Almost 12 percent of the people enrolled in courses for college credit are 35 and older. At commencement time all over the country, newspapers publish pictures of middle-aged mothers in

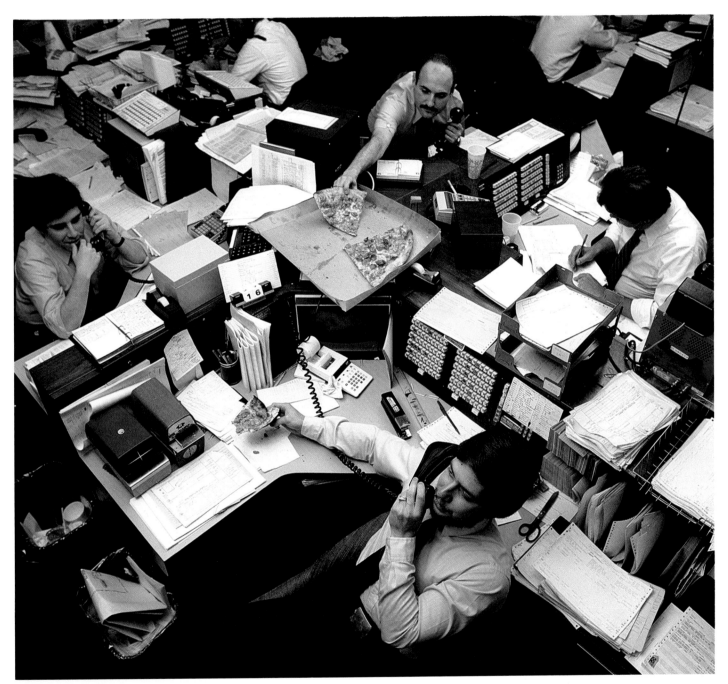

Grabbing a pizza between calls,
traders at a major Wall Street
investment banking firm spare no
time for lunch. Such nonstop workdays
contribute to the high incidence of
heart attacks, ulcers and other stress-
related ailments in the U.S.

6

cap and gown, receiving university diplomas at the same time as their children get their own degrees.

Much of American education is job-oriented, intended to pave the way toward material success. Some 60 percent of the courses studied by adults are taken in order to get a job or advance in a job. Even such renowned centers of scholarship as the University of California and the University of Wisconsin are "land-grant" institutions, founded with government support as colleges stressing the practical arts of agriculture and engineering. But along with such training goes the study of ideals: reliance on individual freedom and responsibility, a need to better the world, a willingness — almost a compulsion — to challenge accepted doctrine. The do-gooders, the dropouts and the rebels as well as the successful entrepreneurs learned their lessons in school. And they, too, fulfill their dreams.

One who did is Kathleen Kinkade. At the age of 34, taking a night course in philosophy at Citrus Junior College in the Los Angeles area, she read *Walden Two*, by the renowned behavioral psychologist B. F. Skinner. It describes a modern utopian community, in which people's responses are reinforced or discouraged by a system of rewards and punishments. This scheme struck Kinkade as "a brilliant flash of light." She read other utopian tracts and the accounts of various 19th-century utopian communities such as Oneida Community in upstate New York. And she resolved to start her own commune.

In 1967 Kinkade, with seven other charter members, raised money for a down payment on a Virginia farmhouse and 100 acres of tobacco fields. Eager but untutored in the ways of farm life, they tried to harvest the to-

bacco crop — with dismal results. Early efforts with cows, then poultry, were equally ineffective; it was cheaper to buy milk and eggs at the supermarket. Yet somehow the commune survived, its 80 members growing most of their own food and bringing in needed cash by weaving hammocks for sale.

"We are still after the big dream," Kinkade says, "a better world, here and now, for as many people as we can manage to support. More, a new kind of human to live in that world: happy, productive, open-minded people who understand that in the long run, human good is a cooperative and not a competitive thing."

Dreams like hers have almost always fallen short. The history of American communes records few long-term successes. Among the better-known utopian communities, Brook Farm lasted about five years, Oneida 30, and New

Harmony 15. So it is, too, with the other dreams, whether of a better society, a different life style or material success. For all those who achieve their goals, there are many who fail. People who, in other cultures, might be content with their lot are lured — even impelled — to pursue what author William James called "the bitch goddess success."

The strains of striving are great, and the social cost is high. If current rates continue, one in every two recent marriages in the U.S. will end in divorce. Drug addiction is a massive problem — four to five million Americans regularly use cocaine. Drug counselors estimate that between half a million and two million people are profoundly dependent on heroin or cocaine. Stress among business executives is so severe that 20 percent of the 500 largest corporations have set up formal programs to help employees cope.

There can be no more embittering experience, particularly for an underprivileged member of society, than to come within reach of the American Dream and be ill-prepared to seize it. This happened to Dwight Johnson, a hero of the Vietnam War.

Johnson grew up in Detroit in a run-down black neighborhood. He never knew his natural father. A bright, skinny boy, whom his mother called Skip, he was often chased home by bullies. "Mama, what do I do if they catch me?" he asked. "Don't you fight, honey," she told Skip, "and don't let them catch you." He became an altar boy and an Explorer Scout and, when he was old enough, a soldier.

It was in Vietnam that his life changed. Assigned to an armored unit, Johnson developed a strong bond with the other men in his tank crew, and he resented an abrupt transfer to another

Moments after receiving their degrees, two gleeful college graduates cavort barefoot in a fountain in New York City. In the mid-1980s, more than a third of all Americans 18 to 20 years old were in college.

tank. The day after his transfer, he was riding down the road with his new crew when they were ambushed. Two of the platoon's four tanks were hit by rockets. When Johnson saw that one was his old tank, he leaped from the turret, ran through the enemy fire to the burning tank and threw open the hatch. He dragged out one badly burned crewman — but before he could go back for his other friends, the tank blew up.

Enraged, Johnson went after the enemy. He killed 20 of them.

"When it was all over," a friend said, "it took three men and three shots of morphine to hold Dwight down."

For his "uncommon valor," Johnson was awarded the Congressional Medal of Honor, the nation's highest award, in a White House ceremony. And then his troubles began.

Johnson was Michigan's only living Medal of Honor winner — and the state, the army and private industry made much of it. He was feted and honored and offered a variety of well-paid jobs. He was given a testimonial dinner attended by 1,500 guests, including General William C. Westmoreland, former commander of U.S. forces in Vietnam. He was lent a costly car, granted credit in stores, and urged to study to become a lawyer; tuition would be paid by the black business community.

He had a great opportunity in his hands, but he was unable to use it. "What does he do when he's introduced to Bunkie Knudsen, the president of Ford?" asked a lawyer friend. "Does he come across strong and dynamic because he knows there is a $75,000-a-year job waiting for him if he makes a good impression? And what happens to him when he just stands there and fumbles and doesn't know if he should shake hands or just nod his head? He was forced to play a role he was never trained for and never anticipated."

The pressure took its toll, physically and emotionally. He told a psychiatrist treating him that the public affairs he had attended had made him feel inadequate. People he met would shake his hand and slap him on the back and tell him to get in touch about a job — yet when he called, he would have to remind them who he was. The costly car lent him was taken away, and he was unable to pay for repairs on a car he purchased for himself, nor could he pay the interest payments on the house he had bought. When his wife had to go to the hospital, he lacked even the $25 deposit that was required.

A few days later Dwight Johnson was shot and killed trying to hold up a store. Said his mother, "Sometimes I wonder if Skip tired of this life and needed someone else to pull the trigger."

That this tragedy struck an impoverished black is understandable. Many of them find the American Dreams beyond reach. A black who did succeed, the prominent New York businessman Lloyd Williams, said once that half the young men with whom he grew up were dead or addicted, or they had vanished. William Beckham Jr., a corporation vice president and a former Assistant Secretary of the Treasury and Deputy Secretary of Transportation, said that in spite of his achievements, he was never able to forget that he was black; white people would not let him. Yet it was also Beckham who said that black Americans are, after all, Americans and that they "buy the American idea."

Roy Levy Williams, a black leader in Detroit, agrees. "Blacks bought into the American Dream even more than whites," he said. "They believe if you work for it in America, you'll get it, or your kids will get it." □

A DIVERSITY OF RELIGIONS

Drawn by the promise of a better life, immigrants to the United States have brought with them not only their hopes but their religions. In a country founded on religious freedom, Americans in turn have created and exported new Christian denominations of their own: Christian Science, Jehovah's Witnesses and the Church of Jesus Christ of Latter-day Saints (the Mormon Church). Christianity remains the dominant religion in this pluralistic society — Roman Catholics number more than 51 million, Protestants more than 73 million. But there are also nearly six million Jews — 40 percent of the world's Jewish population — and about three million Muslims.

Nowhere is the country's religious diversity more readily apparent than in New York City, where there are 1,256 synagogues and 1,766 Protestant, 437 Roman Catholic and 66 Orthodox churches, among others. In one three-mile-square area of Manhattan, as the pictures on these and the following pages reveal, New Yorkers can worship in at least eight different ways.

Friends and family look on as a baby undergoes a Mormon ceremony called "the blessing of the child." Organized in 1830, the Church of Jesus Christ of Latter-day Saints had 3.5 million members in 1985.

While deacons of the church stand by, a man is baptized by total immersion at a Southern Baptist church. With almost 14 million members, the Southern Baptist Convention is the largest Protestant denomination in the country.

Catholics attend Mass in a church copied after Les Invalides in Paris; in the 1980s there were nearly 18,700 Roman Catholic parishes in the country.

Costumed youths perform a drum ceremony called *taiko* in a Buddhist temple hall; there are 150,000 Buddhists in the United States.

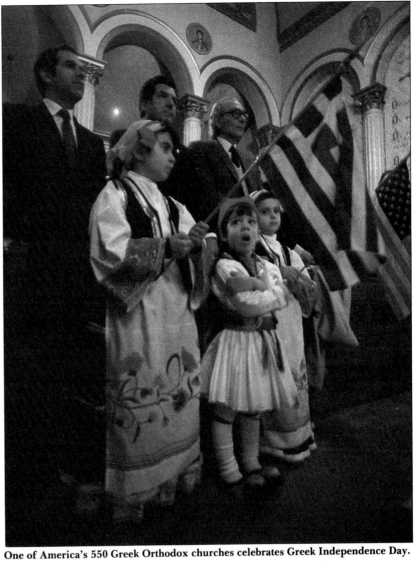

One of America's 550 Greek Orthodox churches celebrates Greek Independence Day.

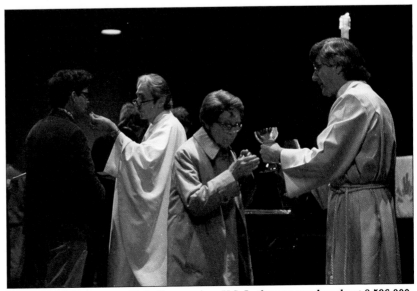

Lutheran ministers serve Holy Communion; U.S. Lutherans number about 8,596,000.

153

A wedding ceremony is performed by a
minister of the Korean United
Church, a Presbyterian denomination.
Presbyterians in the United States
number four million.

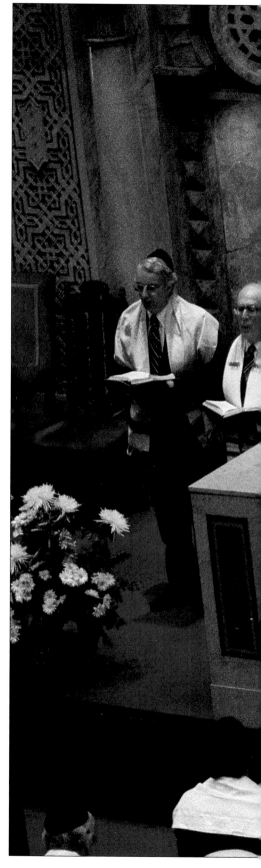

A 13-year-old boy is called up to the
reading of the Torah during his bar
mitzvah, a Jewish ritual denoting
that he has attained religious maturity.
Of the country's six million Jews,
two million live in New York City.

ACKNOWLEDGMENTS

The index for this book was prepared by Barbara L. Klein. For their help in the preparation of this volume, the editors wish to thank: Kate Alfriend, U.S. Dept. of Agriculture, Washington, D.C.; California State Dept. of Agriculture, Sacramento; G. William Domhoff, Adlai E. Stevenson College, University of California, Santa Cruz; Jamie Gipe, Waco, Texas; Joe Goodwin, Washington, D.C.; Vance Grant, Dept. of Education, Washington, D.C.; Kathy Kajari, Chicago Police Dept.; Steve Lawson, Dept. of History, University of South Florida, Tampa; Chuck E. Little, American Land Forum, Bethesda, Md.; Carol Lutyk, National Geographic Society, Washington, D.C.; Major Alex L. Mondragon, Infantry, United States Military Academy, West Point, N.Y.; Kay Mussell, The American University, Washington, D.C.; Dave Nicholl, President, Winterset Chamber of Commerce, Winterset, Iowa; Norman Ornstein, American Enterprise Institute, Washington, D.C.; Wayne D. Rasmussen, U.S. Dept. of Agriculture, Washington, D.C.; John Rorke, Millbrook School, Millbrook, N.Y.

PICTURE CREDITS

Credits from left to right are separated by semicolons, from top to bottom by dashes.

Cover: © Harald Sund. Front and back endpaper maps by: Lloyd K. Townsend. Back endpaper map: Digitized by Creative Data, London.

1, 2: Flag Research Center, Winchester, Massachusetts. 6, 7: John T. Hill, courtesy City Investing Company. 8, 9: Shelly Katz/Black Star, chart digitized by Creative Data, London. 10-13: Nathan Benn/Woodfin Camp, chart digitized by Creative Data, London. 14, 15: George Herben/Woodfin Camp, chart digitized by Creative Data, London. 17: Brown Brothers. 18, 19: Rick Morley/West Stock. 20: © David Muench 1983. 22, 23: Nathan Benn/Woodfin Camp. 24: Barry Kaplan/The Stock Market. 25: Kenneth Garrett/Woodfin Camp. 26, 27: Odyssey Productions/Robert Frerck. 29-35: Winnie Denker. 37: Craig Aurness/West Light. 38: Derosnay/Gamma-Liaison. 39: Tim Thompson. 40-53: Winnie Denker. 54, 55: Jonathan Wallen. 57: Courtesy of The Pennsylvania Academy of the Fine Arts. 58: Library of Congress; except lower left, *Penn's Treaty With The Indians*, Edward Hicks, National Gallery of Art, Washington, D.C., gift of Edgar William and Bernice Chrysler Garbisch 1980. 59: Worcester Art Museum, Worcester, Massachusetts; *Prisoners From The Front*, Winslow Homer, courtesy the Metropolitan Museum of Art, gift of Mrs. Frank B.

Porter 1922 — Alexander Gardner, courtesy Dorothy Meserve Kunhardt Trust. 60: Library of Congress; Wide World Photos; John Olson for *Life* — Courtesy Time Inc. 62: Courtesy of the U.S. Naval Academy Museum. 63: Courtesy the William Turner Collection. 64, 65: Smithsonian Institution National Anthropological Archives, Bureau of American Ethnology Collection. 66: Library of Congress. 68, 69: Winnie Denker. 70, 71: Odyssey Productions/Robert Frerck. 73: Robert Frerck. 74, 76: Chuck O'Rear/West Light. 77: Eric Kroll. 78, 79: William Garnett. 80: Odyssey Productions/Robert Frerck. 82: Maxwell Mackenzie. 84-91: Winnie Denker. 92: From *Jukebox: The Golden Age*, Lancaster Miller & Schnobrich Publishers, Berkeley, California, photograph by Kazuhiro Tsuruta. 94: Henry Groskinsky for *Life*. 95: *Untitled*, Alexander Calder, National Gallery of Art, Washington, D.C., gift of the Collectors Committee 1977. 96: Frank Driggs Collection. 99: Winnie Denker, except upper right: Michael O'Brien/Archive. 101: © 1939 Walt Disney Productions. 102: Courtesy Time Inc. 103: Acme/Wide World. 104: Orlando/Gamma-Liaison. 106-111: Ethan Hoffman/Archive. 112, 113: Nathan Benn. 114, 115: Michael O'Brien/Archive. 116: Nathan Benn/Woodfin Camp. 117: Erich Hartmann/Magnum. 120: The Bancroft Library, University of California, Berkeley. 123: Bill Fitzpatrick/The White House. 124: Wide World Photos. 126-135: Winnie Denker. 136, 137: Michael O'Brien © 1983 National Geographic Society. 138: Odyssey Productions/Robert Frerck. 139: Jose Anzel/Contact Stock Images. 141-145: Max Aguilera Hellweg. 146: Odyssey Productions/Robert Frerck. 147: Katherine Lambert/Black Star. 148: Joan Lifton/Archive. 149: Chuck Fishman. 150-155: Winnie Denker.

BIBLIOGRAPHY

BOOKS

Babcock, C. Merton, *The American Frontier: A Social Literary Record*. Holt, Rinehart and Winston, 1965.

Balliett, Whitney, *Such Sweet Thunder: Forty-Nine Pieces on Jazz*. Bobbs-Merrill, 1966.

Battison, Edwin A., and Patricia Kane, *The American Clock 1725-1865*. New York Graphic Society, 1973.

Bayer, William, *The Great Movies*. Grossett & Dunlap, 1973.

Billington, Ray A., Samuel H. Brockunier and Bert J. Lowenburg, eds., *The Making of American Democracy: Readings and Documents*. Vols. I and II, Rinehart, 1950.

Birdsall, Stephen S., and John W. Florin, *Regional Landscapes of the United States and Canada*. Wiley, 1981.

Boorstin, Daniel J., Brooks Mather Kelley and Ruth Frankel Boorstin, *A History of the United States*. Ginn, 1981.

Buerkle, Jack V., and Danny Barker, *Bourbon Street Black: The New Orleans Black Jazzman*. Oxford University Press, 1973.

Busnar, Gene, *It's Rock 'n' Roll*. Julian Messner, 1979.

Chamberlain, John, *The Enterprising Americans: A Business History of the United States*. Harper & Row, 1963.

Chilton, John, *Who's Who of Jazz*. Chilton, 1972.

Clawson, Marion, *America's Land and Its Uses*. Johns Hopkins, 1972.

Congressional Quarterly:
Editorial Research Reports on America in the 1980s. Congressional Quarterly, 1979.
Editorial Research Reports on American Regionalism. Congressional Quarterly, 1980.
Editorial Research Reports on The Changing American Family. Congressional Quarterly, 1979.
Revolution in Civil Rights. Congressional Quarterly, 1968.

Current, Richard, and John A. Garraty, eds., *Words that Made American History*. Vols. I and II. Little, Brown, 1965.

Dance, Stanley, *The World of Duke Ellington*. Charles Scribner's Sons, 1970.

Davidson, Roger H., and Walter Z. Oleszek, *Congress and Its Members*. Congressional Quarterly, 1981.

Delaunay, Charles, *New Hot Discography: The Standard Directory of Recorded Jazz*. Criterion, 1948.

Detholff, Henry, *Americans and Free Enterprise*. Prentice-Hall, 1979.

Domhoff, G. William, *The Bohemian Grove and Other Retreats*. Harper & Row, 1974.

Dye, Thomas R., *Who's Running America?* Prentice-Hall, 1979.

The Editors of American Heritage Magazine, *American Heritage New Pictorial Encyclopedic Guide to the United States*, Dell, 1965.

Ellington, Edward Kennedy, *Music is My Mistress.* Da Capo, 1976.

Everson, William K., *American Silent Film.* Oxford University Press, 1978.

Fawcett, Edmund, and Tony Thomas, *The American Condition.* Harper & Row, 1982.

Feather, Leonard, *The New Edition of The Encyclopedia of Jazz.* Bonanza, 1960.

Fornatale, Peter, and Joshua E. Mills, *Radio in the Television Age.* Overlook, 1980.

Gabriel, Ralph H., *American Values, Continuity and Change.* Greenwood, 1974.

Garraty, John A., *The American Nation.* American Heritage, 1966.

Garreau, Joel, *The Nine Nations of North America.* Avon, 1981.

Garrow, David J., *Protest at Selma.* Yale University Press, 1978.

Gastil, Raymond D., *Cultural Regions of the United States.* University of Washington Press, 1975.

Gilbert, Annie, *All My Afternoons.* A & W Publishers, 1979.

Graber, Doris A., *Mass Media and American Politics.* Congressional Quarterly, 1980.

Green, Stanley, *The World of Musical Comedy.* A. S. Barnes, 1980.

Harris, H. G., *19th Century American Clocks.* Emerson, 1981.

Head, Sidney W., *Broadcasting in America.* Houghton Mifflin, 1972.

Hofstadter, Richard, *The American Political Tradition.* Vintage/Random House, 1974.

Jablonski, Edward, and Lawrence D. Stewart, *The Gershwin Years.* Doubleday, 1973.

Johnson, E.A.J., and Herman E. Krooss, *The American Economy: Its Origins, Development and Transformation.* Prentice-Hall, 1960.

Jones, Maldwyn Allen, *American Immigration,* University of Chicago Press, 1960.

Kardish, Laurence, *Reel Plastic Magic: A History of Films and Filmmaking in America.* Little, Brown, 1972.

Keynes, Edward, and David Adamany, eds., *The Borzoi Reader in American Politics.* Knopf, 1971.

Kinkade, Kathleen, *A Walden Two Experiment,* Morrow, 1974.

Kramer, Mark, *Making Meat, Milk and Money from the American Soil.* Little, Brown, 1980.

Lahue, Kalton C., *World of Laughter: The Motion Picture Comedy Short, 1919-1930.* University of Oklahoma Press, 1966.

Lahue, Kalton C., and Terry Brewer, *Kops and Custards: The Legend of Keystone Films.* University of Oklahoma Press, 1968.

Least Heat Moon, William, *Blue Highways.* Little, Brown, 1982.

Lipson, Harry A., and John R. Darling, *Marketing Fundamentals: Text and Cases.* Wiley, 1974.

Livesay, Harold C., *American Made: Men Who Shaped the American Economy.* Little, Brown, 1979.

Moore, N. Hudson, *The Old Clock Book.* Tudor, 1936.

Morison, Samuel Eliot, *The Oxford History of the American People.* Vols. I, II and III. New American Library, 1972.

Morrison, Joan, and Charlotte Fox Zabusky, *American Mosaic.* Dutton, 1980.

Nash, Roderick, "American Space," *The American Land.* Smithsonian Exposition Book, 1979.

Newcomb, Horace, *Television: The Critical View.* Oxford University Press, 1976.

Nye, Russel, *The Unembarrassed Muse: The Popular Arts in America.* Dial, 1970.

O'Neill, Thomas, *Back Roads America,* National Geographic Society, 1980.

Ornstein, Norman J., and Shirley Elder, *Interest Groups, Lobbying and Policymaking.* Congressional Quarterly, 1978.

Palmer, Tony, *All You Need Is Love: The Story of Popular Music.* Penguin, 1977.

Parkinson, Michael, and Clyde Jeavons, *A Pictorial History of Westerns.* Hamlyn, 1973.

Poulson, Barry W., *Economic History of the United States.* Macmillan, 1981.

Quint, Howard H., Milton Canton and Dean Albertson, eds., *Main Problems in American History,* Vols. I and II. Dorsey, 1978.

Reeves, Richard, *American Journey.* Simon and Schuster, 1982.

Reid, T. R., *Congressional Odyssey.* W. H. Freeman, 1980.

Roberts, Gene, and David R. Jones, eds., *Assignment America.* Quadrangle/The New York Times, 1974.

Robertson, James Oliver, *American Myth, American Reality.* Hill & Wang, 1980.

Rotkin, Charles, *The U.S.A.: An Aerial Close-up.* Crown, 1968.

Schuller, Gunther, *Early Jazz: Its Roots and Musical Development.* Oxford University Press, 1968.

Schwartz, Charles, *Gershwin: His Life and Music.* Bobbs-Merrill, 1973.

Sheehy, Gail, *Pathfinders.* Morrow, 1981.

Shenton, James P., *History of the United States from 1865 to the Present.* Doubleday, 1964.

Slappey, Sterling G., *Pioneers of American Business.* Grossett & Dunlap, 1973.

Terkel, Studs, *American Dreams, Lost and Found.* Pantheon, 1980.

Wakefield, Dan, *All Her Children.* Doubleday, 1976.

Watson, Richard A., *Promise and Peformance of American Democracy.* Wiley, 1981.

Wilk, Max, *The Golden Age of Television: Notes from the Survivors.* Delacorte, 1976.

Zelinsky, Wilbur, *The Cultural Geography of the United States.* Prentice-Hall, 1973.

PERIODICALS

Agee, James, "Comedy's Greatest Era." *Life,* September 5, 1949.

"American Survey: New York City." *The Economist,* April 2, 1983.

Andersen, Kurt, "The New Ellis Island." *Time,* June 13, 1983.

Batie, Sandra S., and Robert G. Healy, "The Future of American Agriculture." *Scientific American,* February 1983.

Blow, Steve, "Where Dignity Triumphs: Life in Starr County, Texas." *Parade,* May 22, 1983.

Bradshaw, Ted K., "California: Trying Out the Future." *Wilson Quarterly,* Summer 1980.

Cocks, Jay, "American Women: The Climb to Equality." *Time,* July 12, 1982.

"Economic Report of the President." GPO, February 1983.

The Editors of *Wilson Quarterly:*
    "The Changing Family." *Wilson Quarterly,* Winter, 1977.
    "The Public Schools." *Wilson Quarterly,* Autumn, 1979.

Hedberg, Augustin, "How to Change Your Life." *Money,* May 1982.

Henry, William A., III, "Against a Confusion of Tongues." *Time,* June 13, 1983.

"It's Your Turn in the Sun." *Time,* October 16, 1978.

Johnston, Moira, "Silicon Valley — Cradle of the Chip." *National Geographic,* October 1982.

Morgan, Thomas B., "The Latinization of America." *Esquire,* May 1983.

Morganthau, Tom, "America's Small Town Boom." *Newsweek,* July 6, 1981.

"A Portrait of America: Who We Are and How We Are Changing," *Newsweek,* January 17, 1983.

Rawls, James J., "California: Visions and Revisions," *Wilson Quarterly,* Summer 1980.

Thurber, James, "Soapland." *The New Yorker,* May 15, May 29, June 12, July 24, 1948.

Trippett, Frank, "Small Town, U.S.A.: Growing and Groaning." *Time,* September 1, 1980.

U.S. Department of Agriculture, *1983 Fact Book of U.S. Agriculture.* GPO, 1982.

U.S. News & World Report, *The ABC of How Your Government Works.* May 9, 1977.

White, Peter T., "This Land of Ours — How Are We Using It?" *National Geographic,* July 1976.

Woodbridge, Sally B., "The California House." *Wilson Quarterly,* Summer 1980.

INDEX

Time-Life Books Inc. offers a wide range of fine recordings, including a *Big Bands* series. For subscription information, call 1-800-621-7026, or write TIME-LIFE MUSIC, Time & Life Building, Chicago, Illinois 60611.